WALL ART
Wall Paper / Painting / Decoration / Sticker

WALL ART
Wall Paper / Painting / Decoration / Sticker

As an important part of interior and exterior design, a focus on a space sometimes, wall design can tell our tastes, interests and character. No matter what style you fancy, how you design the walls expresses something exciting that has inspired you. In this book, all the works featured are selected from 43 talented design teams worldwide. The cutting-edge designs include various wall-paintings, wallpapers, wall stickers, wall coverings and wall decorations, etc. This book is an invaluable resource of inspiration for professional designers, artists as well as design enthusiasts.

WALL ART
Wall Paper / Painting / Decoration / Sticker

OFFICE

Visual Notes on Synaesthesia	8
Conflicting Disciplines	12
The Collage Wallpaper Series	14
Organic Art	18
Pokobar's Interior Design	20
Rezerwat Vinyli	26
Espacio C Mixcoac	28
Dreamland Wall Installation & Decoration	34
Room Painting of the Designershop "Making Things"	36
Camelia Nedelcu Wall-paintings	38
Faculty of Medicine, University of Baja California	42
Laesart Art School Mural	43
Fantasy Violet	44
Wealthy Walls	45
Waterwolf Wall Design	46

SHOP

D & Me Shop Wall-painting	50
Mimco Dreams Wall Design	54
Pet Point A Pet Store in Tel Aviv	58
Exit Shop & Exit Festival	62
Vipo – Flagship Store, Tel Aviv's Port	64
JUN Street	66
Madam Madsen	68
Mosh Room	70
Wall Art • B & R	73

BAR & RESTAURANT

McDonalds McVillage	74
"Deep" Pub/Cafe	82
Full Space Design for D* Club & Cafe	86
Wall-painting for Black Cat Bar	91
Cristal Bar	92
Teen Action	96
Café El Bache	98
La Voragine Wine Bar	99
Café De La Flor Mural	100
Australian Vine House	102
Energy 2000	106
Offside Interior	110
Berry Hill "Uth" Center	114
Canvas Bar	116

EXHIBIT

Fun-occult	120
Buckminster-Fullerene Dream	122
Art of Persuading Exhibition Entrance Room	126
Exhibition Design Torture Basement	128
Reykjavik Art Museum	132
Matisse &	137
Arena Wall-painting	138
Red Blue Motion Totem 2010	140
Colour State	142
Club Trouw Amsterdam III	146
Roger Mercury	148
Graphic Interpretation of Vlissingen	150
Glasgow People	152
An Emphatic YES!	154
Talking about My Spontaneous Generation	156

RESIDENCE

Peonies, Lilies & Other Pretties	162
Walt Disney Signature	166
Masters Anniversary Edition	167
Stacy Garcia Luxury Wallpapers	168
Medley Design	170
Contracted Wallpaper	171
Gorgeous Wallpaper	172
Walk in the Park Wallpaper	174
Vintage Wallpaper	175
Sumptuous Wallpaper	176
Natural Wallpaper	177
Pompadour Wallpapers	178
Aimee Wilder Wallpaper	180
Circle Art	185
Svärmor Wallpapers	186
Lady of Easy Virtue	188
News	189
La Vie En Rose & Rosmarie	190
Baronessa	191
N-pool	192
Point36.6	194
Midia Effects Design Studio	196
Alice in Dreamland	198
Wall-painting	198
E-glue	200
Viernes De Animas Movie Set	208
Mural Gris	210
Mural Azul	211
Golden Drops	212
Naive	214
Wall-painting of Bizarre Animals	216
Wall-painting & Collage Art	217
Lovely Wall Sticker Designs	220
Sticker: Metre, Life, Branches, Floreal & Okapi	223

CONCEPT

Patterns for Wall Decoration	226

Visual Notes on Synaesthesia

Completion Date: November, 2008
Designers: Elizabeth Corkery
Photographer: Chloe Hughes
Client: Independent Art Installation

Visual Notes on Synaesthesia is a printed installation that draws inspiration from what Elizabeth describes as the "language of synaesthesia". Synaesthesia is a neurological condition that results in the combining of one or more senses; colours can be tasted or words felt against the skin like objects.

Through extensive research and the accumulation of anecdotal evidence, scientists have been able to identify a set of "form constants"; shapes and patterns are universal across the diverse range of synaesthetic experience. These constants include, rigid geometric shapes and repeat patterns, spirals, sunbursts, honeycomb shapes, and dots. The result of this inspiration is the environment where surfaces have been affected by these synaesthetic forms and exist somewhere between the familiar and the irrational.

The installation is made up of framed, original screenprints, printed textile and screenprinted wall panels. The installation existed as a temporary environment, and is only represented now through its photo documentation.

Conflicting Disciplines

Completion Date: 2008
Designer: Egor Kraft
Photographers: Olga Vasilenko, Egor Kraft

An idea of the conflicting disciplines mural is to illustrate the contradictions using a collage of visual languages of an epoch of the renaissance and a modernism, esthetic values of a classical antiquity and force of gesture of action painting. Realistically drawn David's head and a column of the corinthian order are covered with carelessly imposed spontaneous dabs of paint. The work also aimed at reducing of excessive neatness and clearness of all the interior in general by involving bright colours and creating visual and meaningful conflict on the wall of apartment based in the historical center of St. Petersburg.

The Collage Wallpaper Series

Completion Date: 2010
Designer: Brunella Giannangeli
Photographer: Marta Bahillo
Client: The Galatea Studio

The collage wallpaper series is a collection of wall-coverings stemming from a harmonic composition of various elements. Fusing collage and illustration techniques, the collection not only features a modern aesthetic, but also hints at a retro feel with its applied vintage hairstyles. This print series is rich in graphic details and allows textures to play an important role in order to achieve its purpose.

Organic Art

Completion Date: January 2008
Designer: Sandy Howard
Photographer: Steve Pell

While art usually hangs on the wall, sometimes art is the wall. Illustrator Sandy Howard has a passion for filling her time with mehndi-inspired works. Rather than limiting herself to a canvas, Sandy challenges her art by illustrating on walls, purses, notebooks and even shoes! Living in a primer-covered white loft, Sandy and her partner Steve Pell, decided that their foyer wall was too bare. They had a price estimate for installing patterned wallpaper, but at $450(can), so they decided that they could paint their own wall.

The total completed cost of the mural was a mere $3(can), after she had a coupon to save money on the paint tube, and used a paintbrush she's had since childhood. Sandy hopes the mural will inspire others to create beauty simply for the sake of creating beauty. Her artistic motto encourages artists to "work with what you've got".

Pokobar's Interior Design

Completion Date: 2009
Designer: Branimir Sabljić
Photographer: Branimir Sabljić
Client: Pokobar, Full Service Advertising Agency

In Zagreb city downtown, an apartment of 180 square meters was turned into an office space for three sister companies. As rooms are divided according to function, the artist decided to express by explicit naming of room functions using Hypertrophed typography. The effect of "indoor graffiti" transforms the segmented apartment into a public space where business is conducted, while retaining a frivolous styling used by creative professionals. Variations of styling of different rooms not only show function but also set the mood by a combination of hand painting and disruption of straight wall lines and angles.

• Wall Art • Office •

22

Rezerwat Vinyli

Completion Date: 2009
Designers: Nawer & Pan1ka
Photographer: Olga Borda
Client: Senor Soul

Coffee bar concept vinyl store has an extraordinary characteristic atmosphere similar to no other in Krakow. It not only offers great coffee and the typical services of a cafe, but also provides wonderful place where visitors can relax to the sound of good music served by the play of Vinyl Records, which can also be purchased for your home collection.

The interior design begins with the juxtaposition of two wall mounted graphics that colourfully spread along the surface of the wall connecting to other interior elements, such as lighting, furniture and the building structure ultimately producing a coherent whole within the space.

Espacio C Mixcoac

Completion Date: July 2009
Design Firm: ROW Studio
Designers: Álvaro Hernández Félix,
Nadia Hernández Félix,
Alfonso Maldonado Ochoa
Photographer: Juan Marcos Castañeda
Client: Coca Cola FEMSA

The first training facility called Espacio C (C Space - C for the initials of Coca Cola, Training, Quality, Commitment and Creativity in Spanish) is located at the Mixcoac Distribution Center on the southwestern area of Mexico City.

It includes three separate rooms that can be joined together for common activities, a mediateque, snacks bar, souvenir store, data and electrical connections and storage space. The brief also required to include elements from the different brands of Coca Cola FEMSA and to reinforce the company's values in the space.

These spaces are surrounded by a wall that acts as a sound and visual barrier that isolates the training facility from the city and the rest of the areas of the plant. The wall was thought as a continuous surface on its outer side that folds to the floor and ceiling. The walls and ceiling have a Coca Cola red epoxy paint coating and the floor is finished with a high resistance acrylic finish.

The interior walls are covered with a special anti graffiti coating that turns the full surface of the wall into a dry erase board and at the same time encapsulates the vinyl graphics protecting them from damage. This project was awarded with a Merit Award on the 2009 Best of Year Awards of Interior Design Magazine, on a ceremony at the Solomon R. Guggenheim Museum in New York in 2009.

31

33

- Wall Art
- Office

Dreamland Wall Installation & Decoration

Completion Date: 2007
Design Firm: Undoboy
Photographer: Undoboy
Client: Blik, Undoboy

This set of wall graphics was designed by Undoboy. The cute patterns and elements in bright colours featured in the works created a relaxed and pleasant atmosphere for the rooms, and brought a style which is interesting and memorable. The works shown in right page were created for a time-lapse video of wall installation.

Room Painting of the Designershop "Making Things"

Patric Sandri Illustration was asked to paint these works in the space. The designers just adopted Acrylic black to draw freely and arbitrarily on the wall and the ceiling. The wall-painting in graffiti style shows us an infinite imaginary world with abstract figures, animals and plants. These unique and bizarre images make the small room full of childishness and playfulness. These abstract images which seem to be ruleless and irregular turn out to present us a limitless space for the limited room.

Completion Date: 2009
Design Firm: Patric Sandri Illustration
Photographer: Patric Sandri
Client: Making Things

Camelia Nedelcu Wall-paintings

Completion Date: 2009
Design Firm: Camelia Nedelcu
Client: Different firms

This free hand painting with free subject selects brown and yellow as the major hue of the work. Even though the pattern design seems to be not very complex without any stagy decorating, but it presents comfortable and fantastic feeling for the plain space. A vogue woman's face, some abstract patterns and magic graffities, all these creations on the wall reflect a style that is both meaningful and identifiable.

39

- Wall Art • Office •

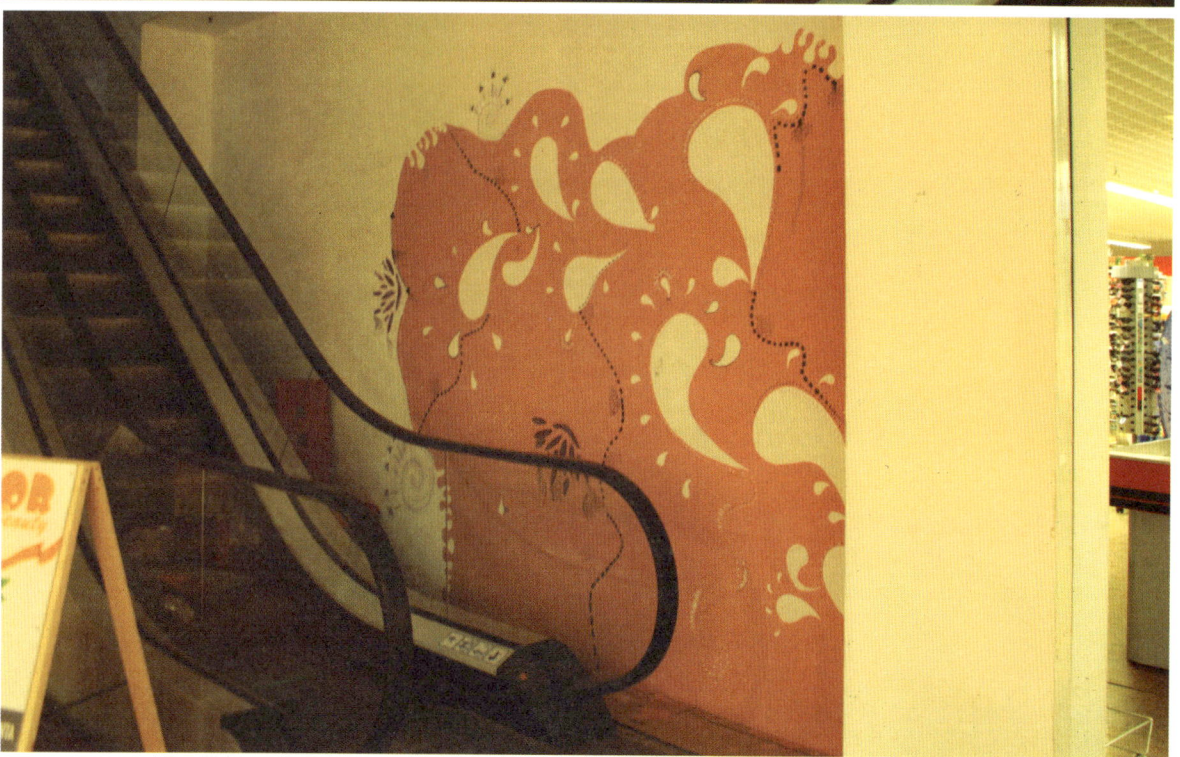

40

41

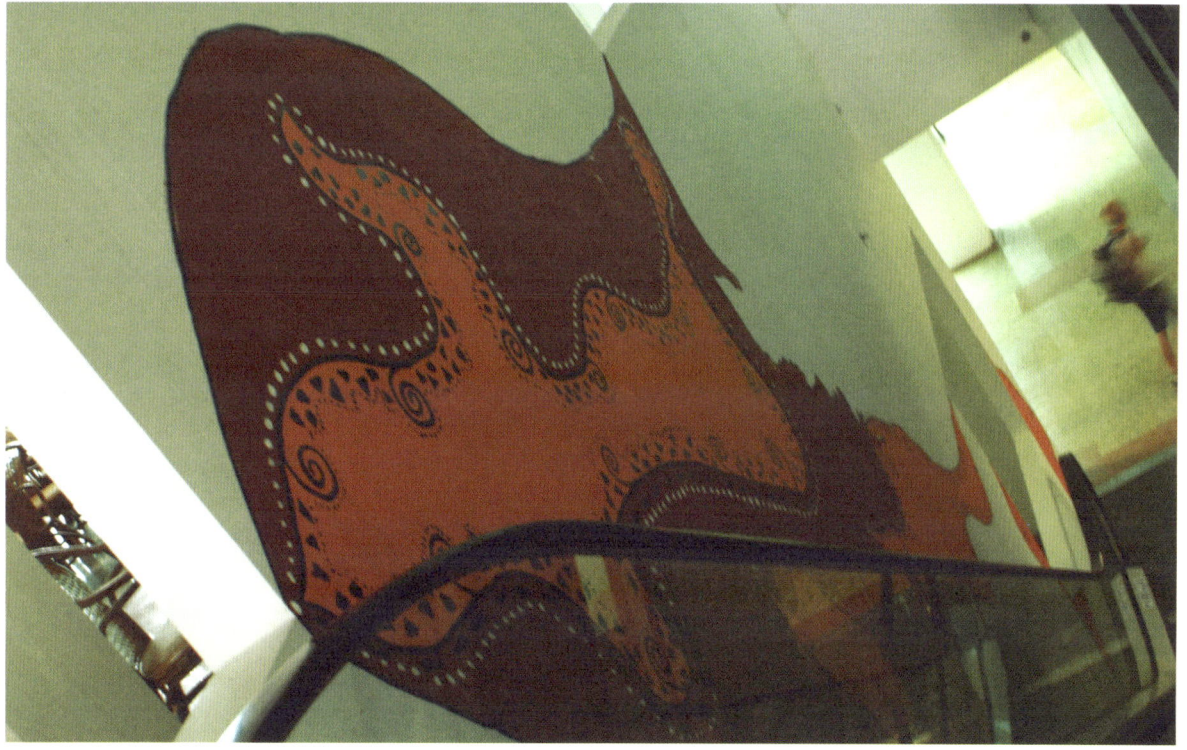

Faculty of Medicine, University of Baja California

Completion Date: 2008
Designer: Victor Sandoval
Photographer: Victor Sandova
Client: University of Baja California

The mural was created for the medicine faculty in one of the most important universities in California, USA. It is a mural depicting a dance between life and death and in the middle is the new beginning or new life. The plants on the sidelines are medicinal Aztec plants and also in the background are the mourners of those have passed. This is an important mural, not only for the location, but also the different meanings that lay underneath.

Laesart Art School Mural

Completion Date: 2009
Designer: Victor Sandoval
Photographer: Victor Sandova
Client: Laesart Art School

A two-story mural depicting the famed Don Quixote de la Mancha speaking words of unity and brotherhood in different symbols and the eyes express the sadness of a dreamer.

Painted in acrylic paints and stencil, this mural stands in the center of the building of Bauhaus inspiration where all the windows face toward the center patio.

Fantasy Violet

Completion Date: 2009
Designer: Olefir Zoya
Client: Design Studio "STYLE"

The aesthetic centre in the design studio "STYLE" is a decorative wall which divides the room into two working spaces. This wall has become the "Morning Coat" of the design studio. It is a bright spot in the interior in monochrome and neutral colours.

Desire to create emotions and to transmit a strong sense of style are the main task of this wall.

A lot of decorative elements, shapes, relief, crystal and gold in the basis of fantasy violet open the space for inspiration and imagination.

Wealthy Walls

Completion Date: August 2007
Designer: Wendy Plovmand
Client: Wallcollection DK

Wealthywalls is a highly exclusive wallpaper designed for people and places daring extreme wealthiness in everyday life. The title refers to the detailed illustration and the price while it encompasses reference to the decadence and overindulgence of high society living.

Waterwolf Wall Design

Completion Date: 2007
Designers: Trapped in Suburbia
Client: Waterwolf

A laboratorium for social experiments, Waterwolf's interior was designed as a space filled with energy, dynamism and passion with the illustrated graphics on the wall, blending the spirit of science and times. The immersive colours, exaggerated letters and some modern characters created a happy and exuberant environment within the space.

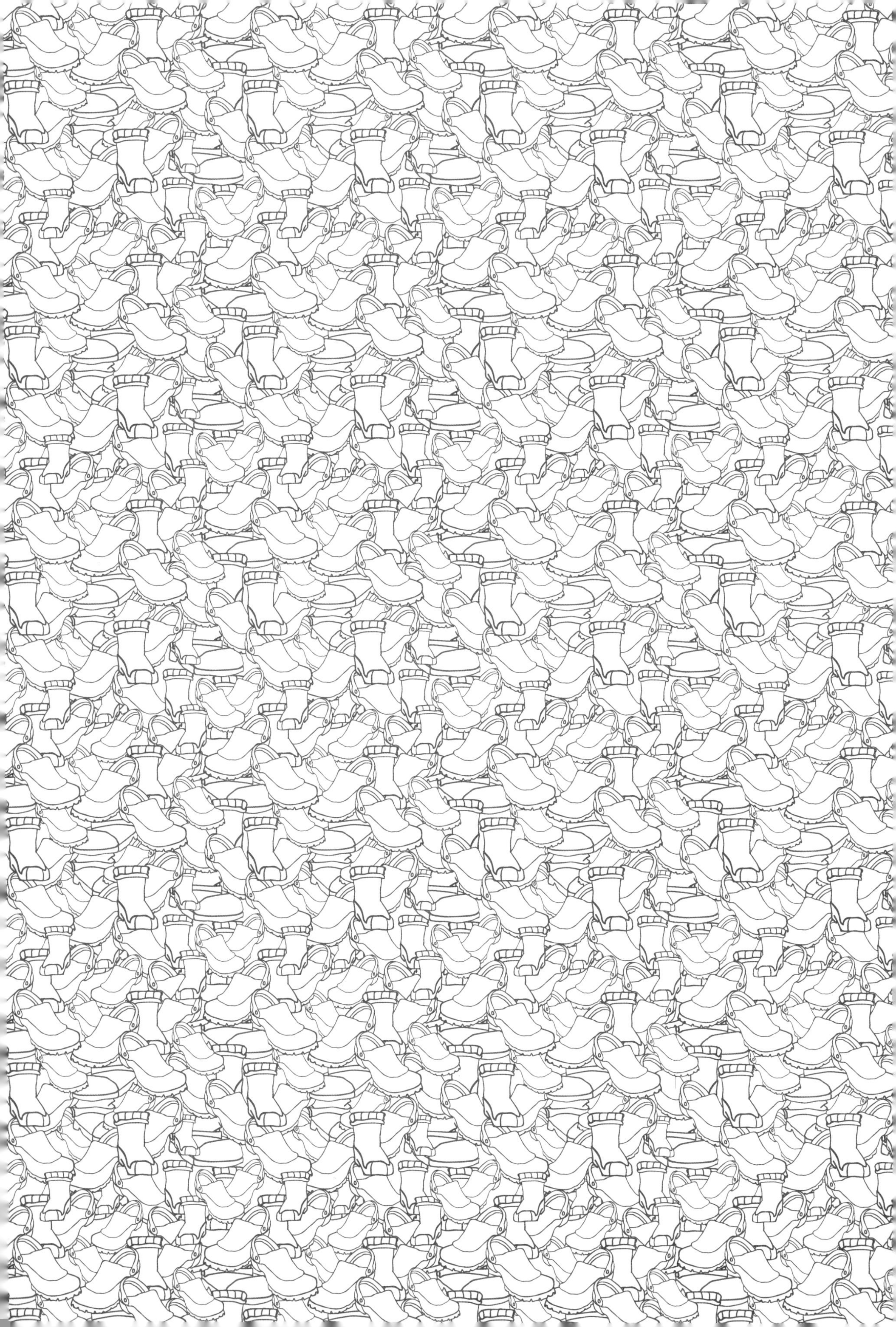

Wall Art • Shop

D & Me Shop
Wall-painting

Completion Date: September 2009
Design Firm: Miss Led Illustration
Designer: Joanna Henly
Photographer: Derek Bremner
Client: Mimco

This is a great project as the only limitations were time! The designer had two weeks to complete as much wall space as possible over 3 floors, adjoining staircases, corridors, doors and changing rooms!

The works were produced from sketches created before and during the project. As it is a unique feminine mix of new and vintage clothing and accessories, Joanna wanted to portray that in her illustration work using influences from various times and places through a contemporary delivery.

Using the architectural detailing over the three floors the images are seen along pathways, where flowers or cloud elements entice you further towards the beguiling feminine characters. Creating a wonderland of beauty and sensuality female shoppers were invited into an environment of fantasy and play, a very good marketing tool!

You dint seen Nothing Yet.

Wall Art • Shop

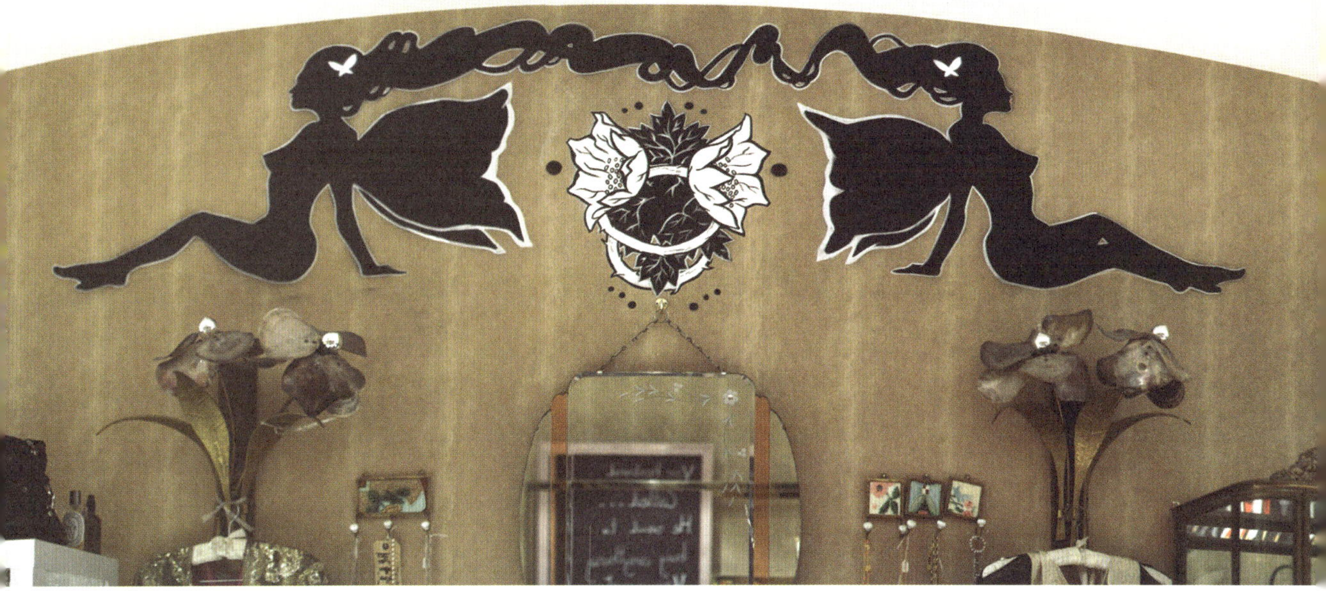

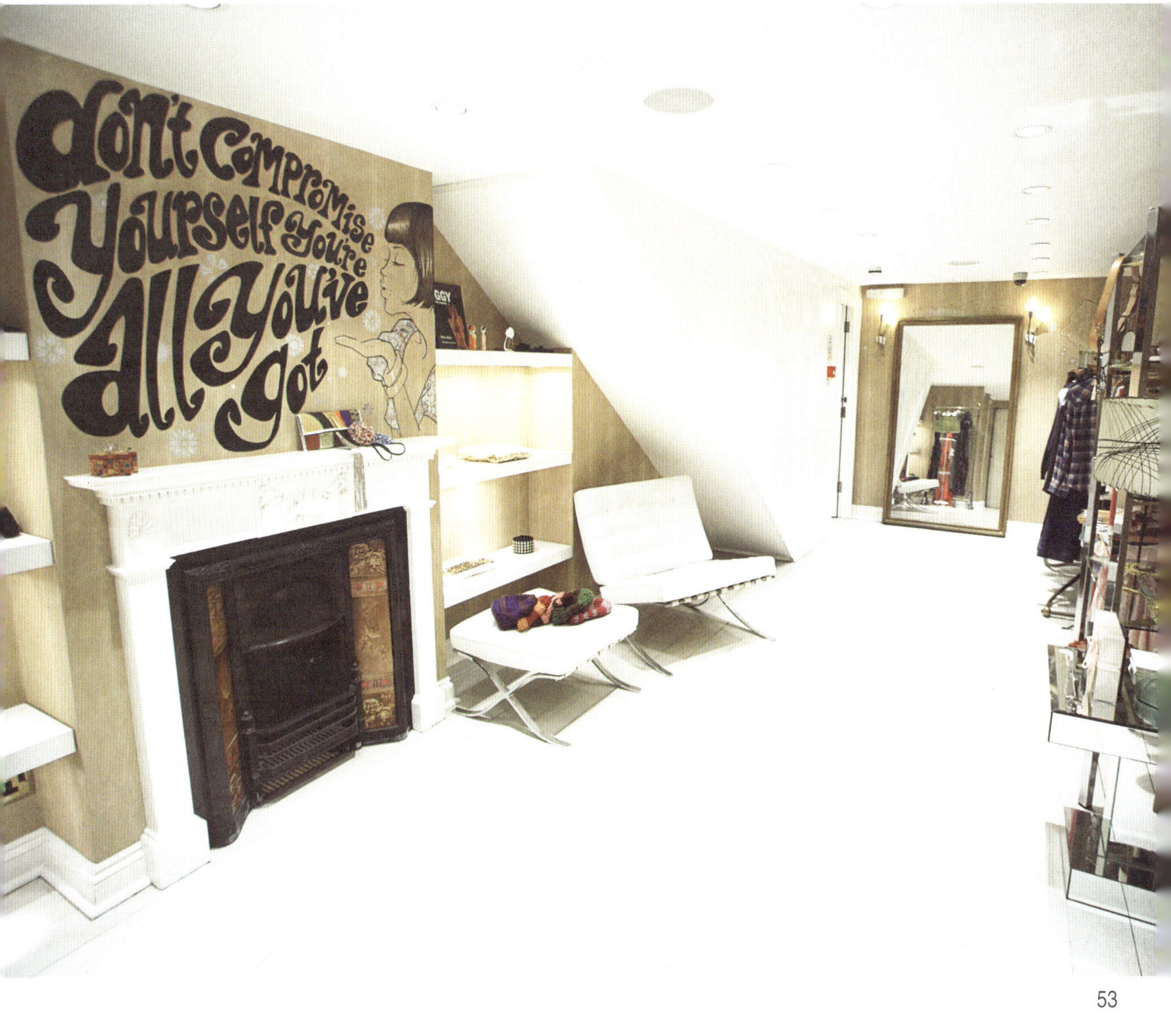
don't compromise yourself you're all you've got

Mimco Dreams Wall Design

Completion Date: April 2010
Design Firm: Miss Led Illustration
Designer: Joanna Henly
Photographer: Derek Bremner
Client: Mimco
Main materials: Aerosol Paint, Acrylic, Paint Pens on Board

Mimco Boutique, sitting amidst the delectable cutting edge hair salons, high class café's and restaurants on the cobbled streets of Covent Garden are wonderfully bejou and neat. The space filled with accessories, bags and shoes set against a backdrop of light slate grey, which calling out for some colour and excitement.

The designer was commissioned to fill the empty wall, which is seen by shoppers and passes-by through the main window. The idea was to create a "Miss Led" lady adorned in Mimco's products with some interesting elements giving the final piece a bit of a twist. Not only to highlight the key designs fashioned on an eclectic and stylish model but also to highlight the theme of "more is more".

They decided on creating a sugary sweet and floaty feel which contrasted against large fairytale style bugs and dark beetles. For such a feminine piece it called for very clean brush outlines, very graf art inspired. Juxtaposed against the perfected lines were thin washes of grey and brown poured over the piece to add a sense of ageing to tie in with the fashion conscious concept.

The Essence of **MIMCO**

Mimco was born in 1996 in Melbourne, Australia. We **dream**, **explore** & **play** with whatever gives us **delight** in the moment.

to **dress up** & she knows
kes to her look
is on the
the

ration in & w n we
for what w D, so
desire.

ore, interac llow
yourself.

• Wall Art • Shop •

57

Pet Point
A Pet Store in Tel Aviv

Completion Date: 2009
Design Firm: Miss Lee Design
Designer: Lee-Ran Shlomi Gidron
Photographers: Dor Shlomi
Client: S.S Animal ltd.

A pet store in "Ha'hashmonaim" street, a busy street in central Tel Aviv. As a store designed for pet "Supermarket", this project required branding the walls of the store in order to create a shopping environment, and to strengthen the brand's image. The walls were wrapped in graphics inspired by street art that communicates with the customers throughout the store, wherever they are. Each section of the store is characterized by different graphics, matching the type of product being sold in that section.

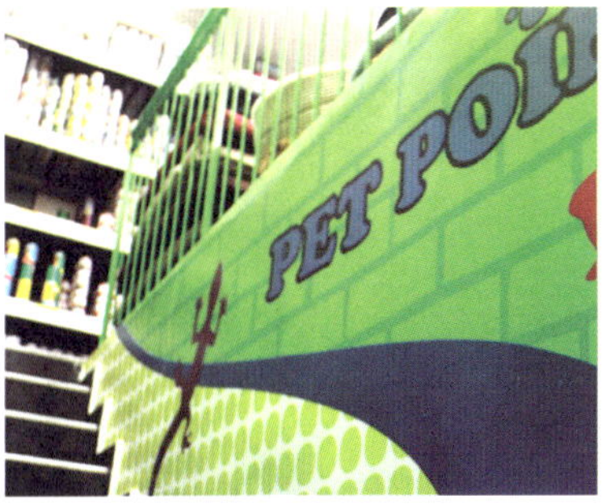
PET POI

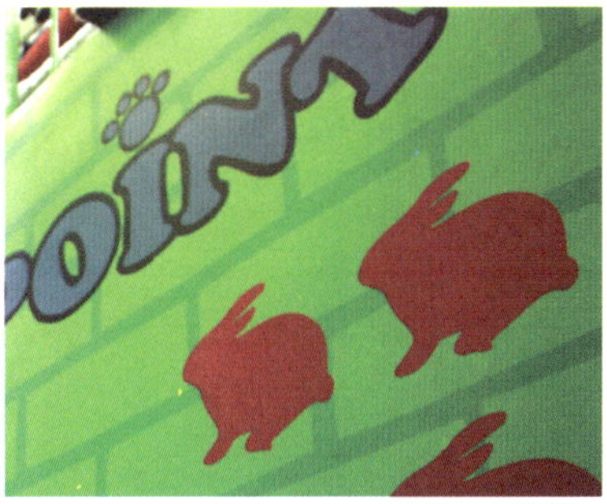

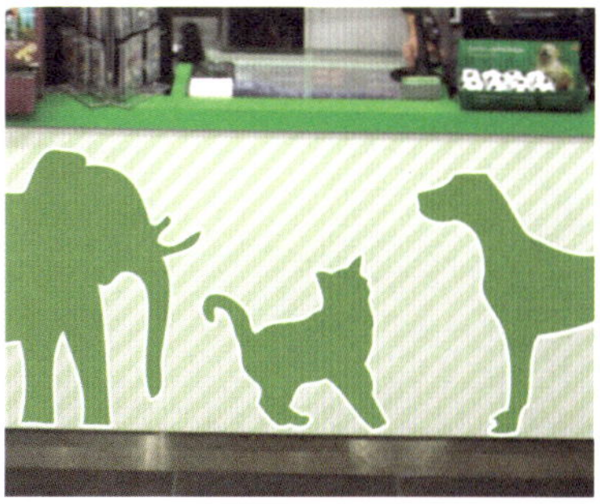

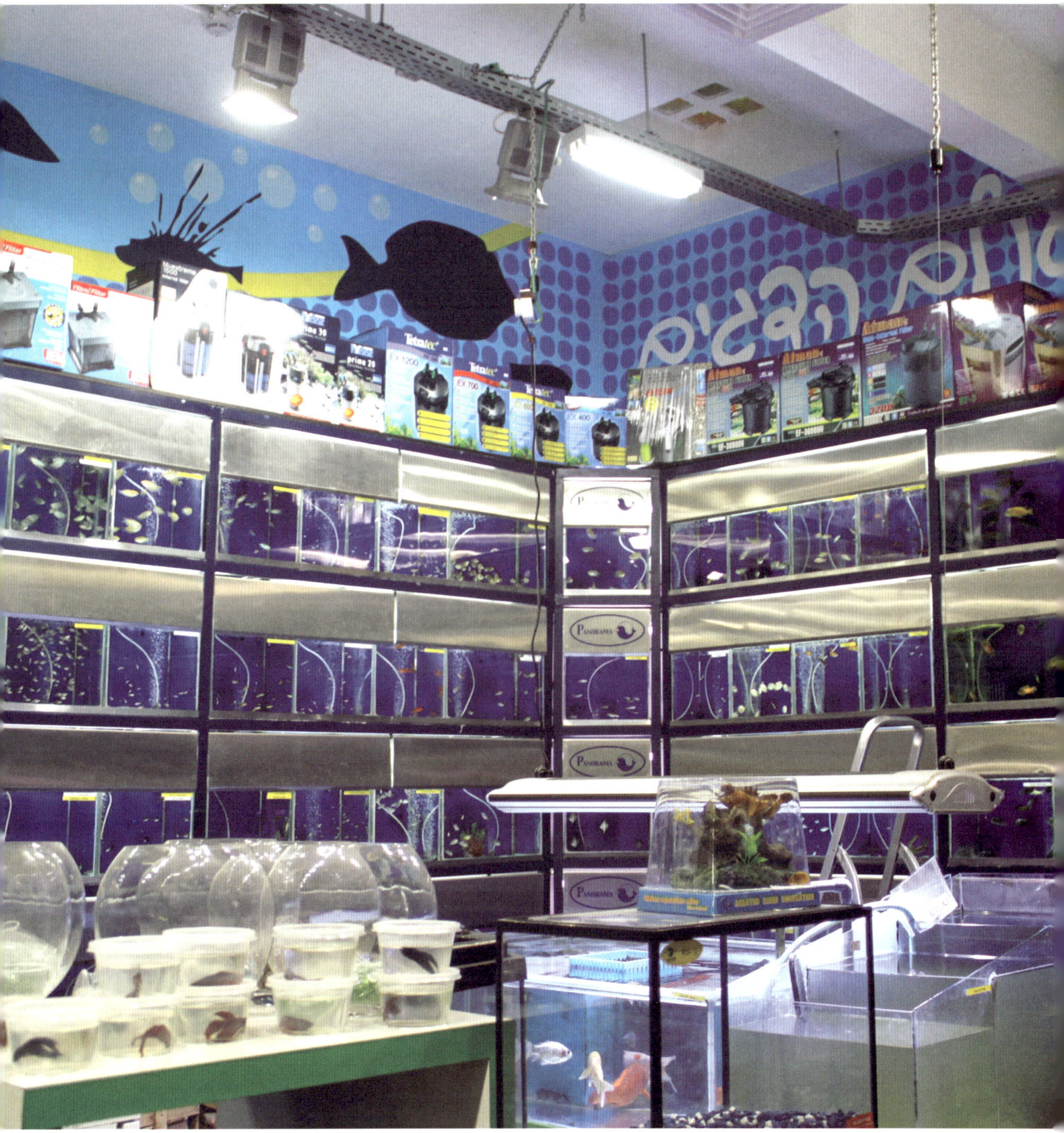
Tetratec
EX 1200
EX 700
EX 400
prima 20
PANORAMA

- Wall Art
- Shop

61

Exit Shop & Exit Festival

Completion Date: 2009
Design: D-bend Design Studio
Photography: D-bend Design Studio

D-Bend Design Studio was asked to design the interior with a background wall for Shop on Festival where their visual identity was evolved into the installation made of recycled materials .

The dynamic visual identity for Exit Festival`s Online Shop and Shop on Festival is a main element for this space. The theme of Exit Festival 2009 is Recycling so they came up with the logo that represents recydeing idea.

The identity logo transforms in various patterns and shapes which are later accompanied with loads of different characters representing the festival crowd and festival experience in general.

63

Vipo – Flagship Store, Tel Aviv's Port

Completion Date: 2009
Design Firm: Miss Lee Design, Toolbox-design
Designers: Lee-Ran Shlomi, Itay Gidron, Yaron Kanor
Photographer: Ya-Lee
Client: Vipo Land GmbH / Globe International Holdings S.A.

This toy store is based on the international TV series "Vipo – the Adventures of a Flying Dog". On this project, the designers wanted to illustrate a scene from the animated series, Vipo the flying Dog and allow children to experience the world of Vipo, get closer, touch the characters, watch the show and play "Vipo" computer games. When you enter the store, it seems as though you have been thrown into one of the episodes, and the children are the stars of the show.

Every part of the store was utilized in an optimal way in order to create a rich and fascinating experience for the children.

65

JUN Street

Completion Date: 2009
Design Firm: Kingdrips
Designer: Andreas Klammt
Client: Carhartt

Kingdrips was commissioned by Carhartt to produce a colourful illustration for window decoration of the Jun street wear store in Hamburg city.

The Leaves through the citylandscape where people meet everyday are a main element in the work. Falling of colourful leaves, spreading of natural colours and growing of leaves, all these concepts reflect the brand identity.

Wall Art • Shop

67

Madam Madsen

Completion Date: 2009
Design Firm: Tim Bjørn Design Studio
Designer: Tim Bjørn
Client: Madam Madsen

There are illustration and custom typography for wall design of Madam Madsen shop. The things you can buy are things for decorating your home kept in a romantic style, and Tim has to somehow reflect that in the illustration.

The illustrated trees are symbols of joy, awareness, music, love and secrets which are all part of life, summing up the way you decorate your home and telling a story about you as a person.

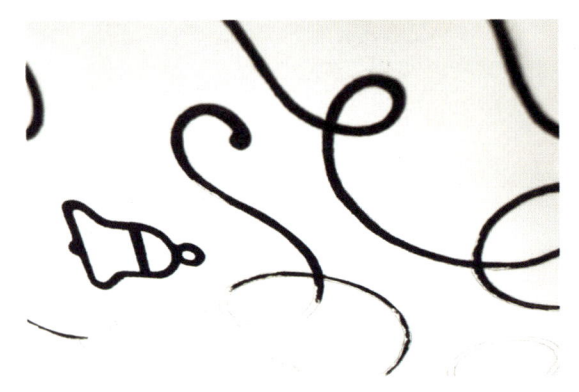

- Wall Art
- Shop

Madam Madsen

Mosh Room

Completion Date: November 2006
Designers: Wendy Plovmand, Kasper Hammer
Photographer: Anne Mie Dreves
Client: Normann Copenhagen

A brilliant illustration and light design installation were created for the design store of Normann Copenhagen which is a famous brand offering creative products.

All the works were created by experimenting with light and visual graphics. The design refers to a wild colliding dance and the magic hallucination, playing with scale and perspective. The cutting-edge style of the work matches the brand perfectly.

71

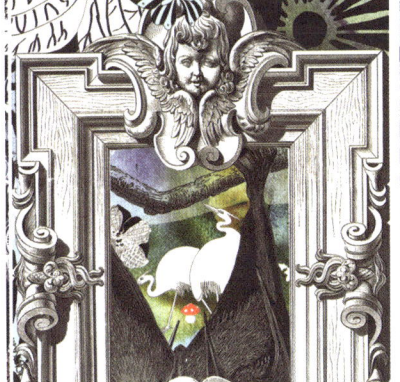

Wall Art • B & R

McDonalds McVillage

Completion Date: November 2008
Designer: UXUS
Photographer: Dim Balsem
Client: McDonalds Europe

Mcdonald's commissioned UXUS to create an inspiring children's activity area for kids under 7 years of age, bringing the theme of "what I eat, what I do" to life. The concept embodies an inspiring, playful, educational and entertaining area within a Mcdonald's restaurants which is no bigger than 20m^2 in the space.

The entire Mcdonalds project is a spatial application of graphic design. The aesthetic is playful, yet visually sophisticated, designed to enhance the overall atmosphere of the restaurant and please both the parents and children.

The experience consists of a series of "cottages" with simple activities where kids can stimulate their imagination and "cook" up their own stories and games; a make-believe Mcdonald's "village" or simply put "the mcvillage". The use of images instead of words transcends those barriers associated with different geographical areas and children's ages.

Each "cottage" represents a phase of the journey food going through before finally arriving at the dinner table. Their journey starts on the "farm", goes to the "market" and finally ends up at the "kitchen". The cottages are designed to house simple activities that will engage children in a physically playful manner, communicating to them a positive message about eating or making food in a fun and stimulating way.

Special attention was paid to the use of durable materials that can withstand the heavy usage. They also needed to be nontoxic and the colours last for a long time. Through the use of mostly graphics combined with selected 3D play elements UXUS creates one story which seeks to capture their imagination by presenting scenarios in which they become the "character" of a certain activity: chefs in the kitchen; clerks at the market and farmers at the farm.

75

- Wall Art • Bar & Restaurant •

76

77

- Wall Art
- Bar & Restaurant

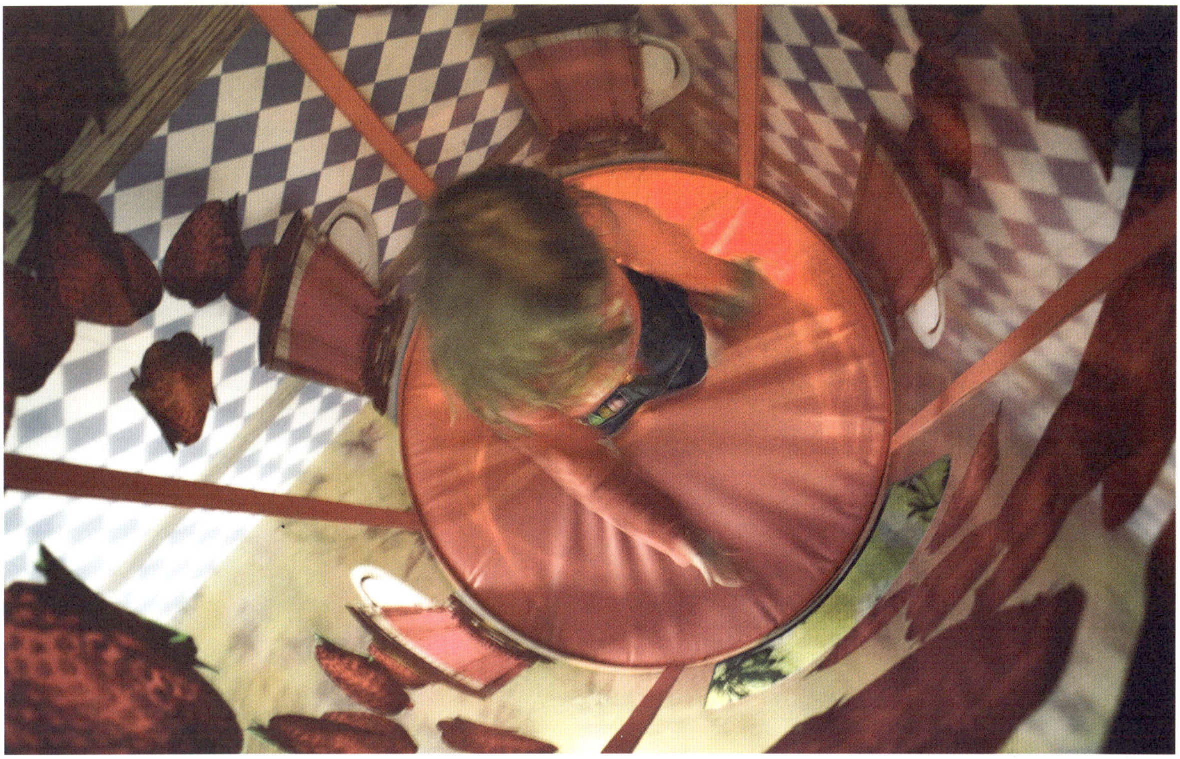

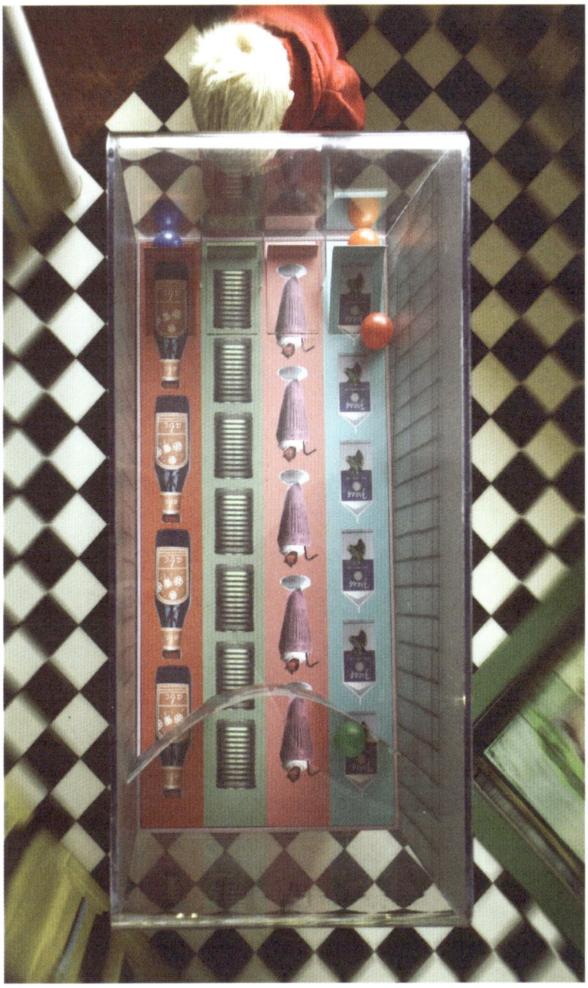

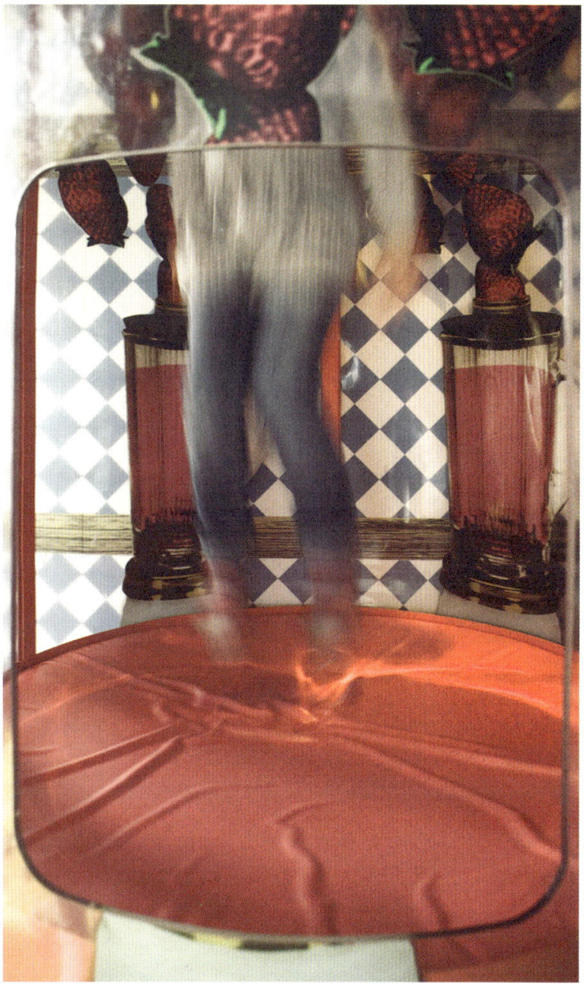

• Wall Art • Bar & Restaurant •

80

81

"Deep" Pub/Cafe

This is an interior design and wall-paintings for newly opened "Deep" Pub/Cafe, located in Belgrade, Serbia. This piece of splendid wall-painting adopts the orange as one of the basic colour, which creates a warmer and milder atmosphere under the light. Especially, the city silhouette, a reversed image on the top of the wall builds an illusion of night scene. The misty atmosphere matches this pub or cafe perfectly and gives a sense of warmth. Besides, the lovely giraffe at the porch, the vivid motorbike, the hand-drawn back of a walking man with a guitar, the inverted back above the tiny table and the group of instruments, all these lovely elements bring an unlimited feeling of interesting and cordiality to the plain and limited space.

Completion Date: 2008
Design Firm: Skills Division
Designer: Saša Ivanović
Photographer: Skills Division
Client: "Deep" Pub/Cafe

83

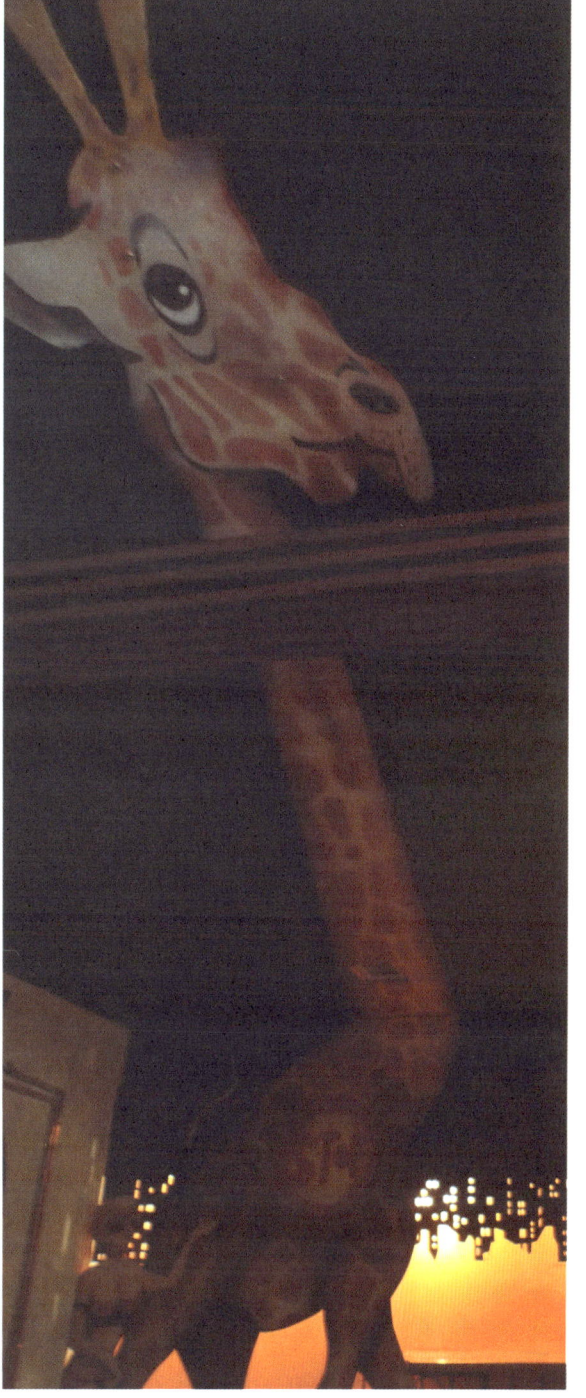

- Wall Art • Bar & Restaurant •

84

85

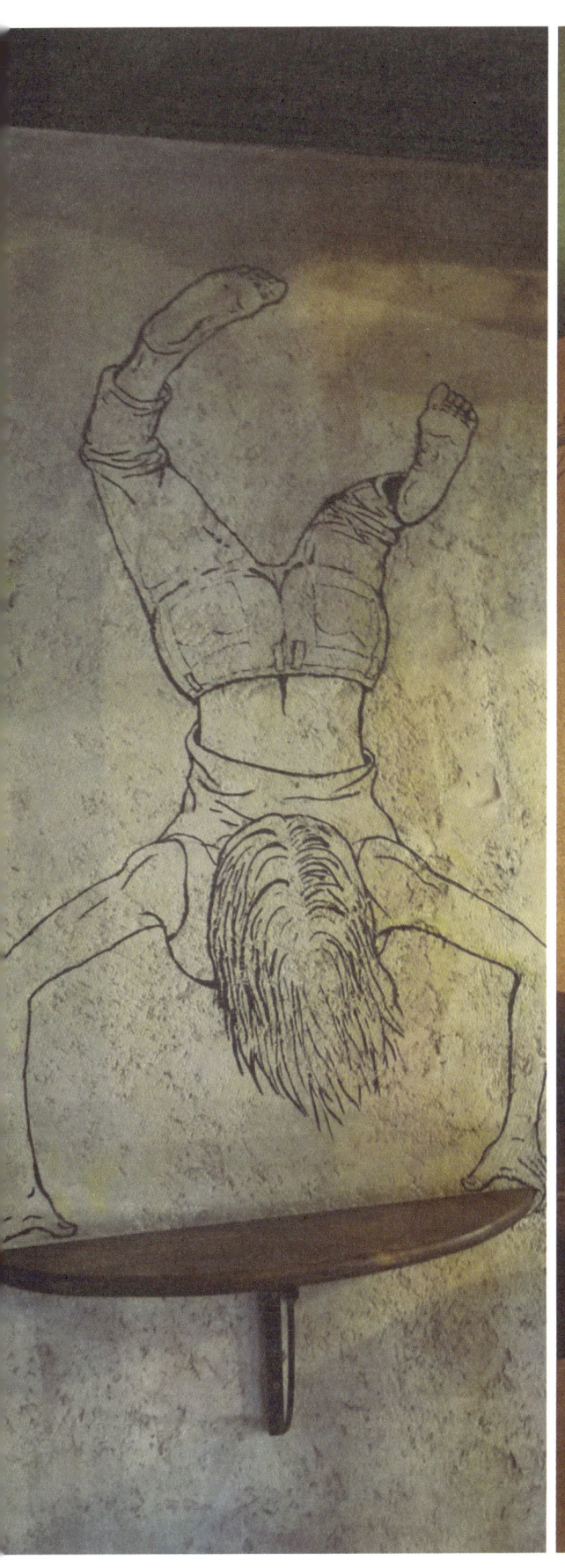

Full Space Design for D* Club & Cafe

Completion Date: 2009
Design Firm: Dopludó Collective,
Designers: Aleksey Galkin,
Eibatova Karina, Egor Kraft
Photographers: Egor Kraft, Aleksey Galkin
Client: D* Club & Cafe

This is full space design for D* Club & Cafe, a small cozy club and cafe on the Gulf of Finland in street Petersburg.

Some features in the space are semicircular shapes and smooth transitions instead of a corner between the walls and ceiling. The black murals on white walls look very modern and elegant, showing various illustrated images such as magic fairy tales, northern folk elements and mystical creatures on the walls, ceiling and columns in the space.

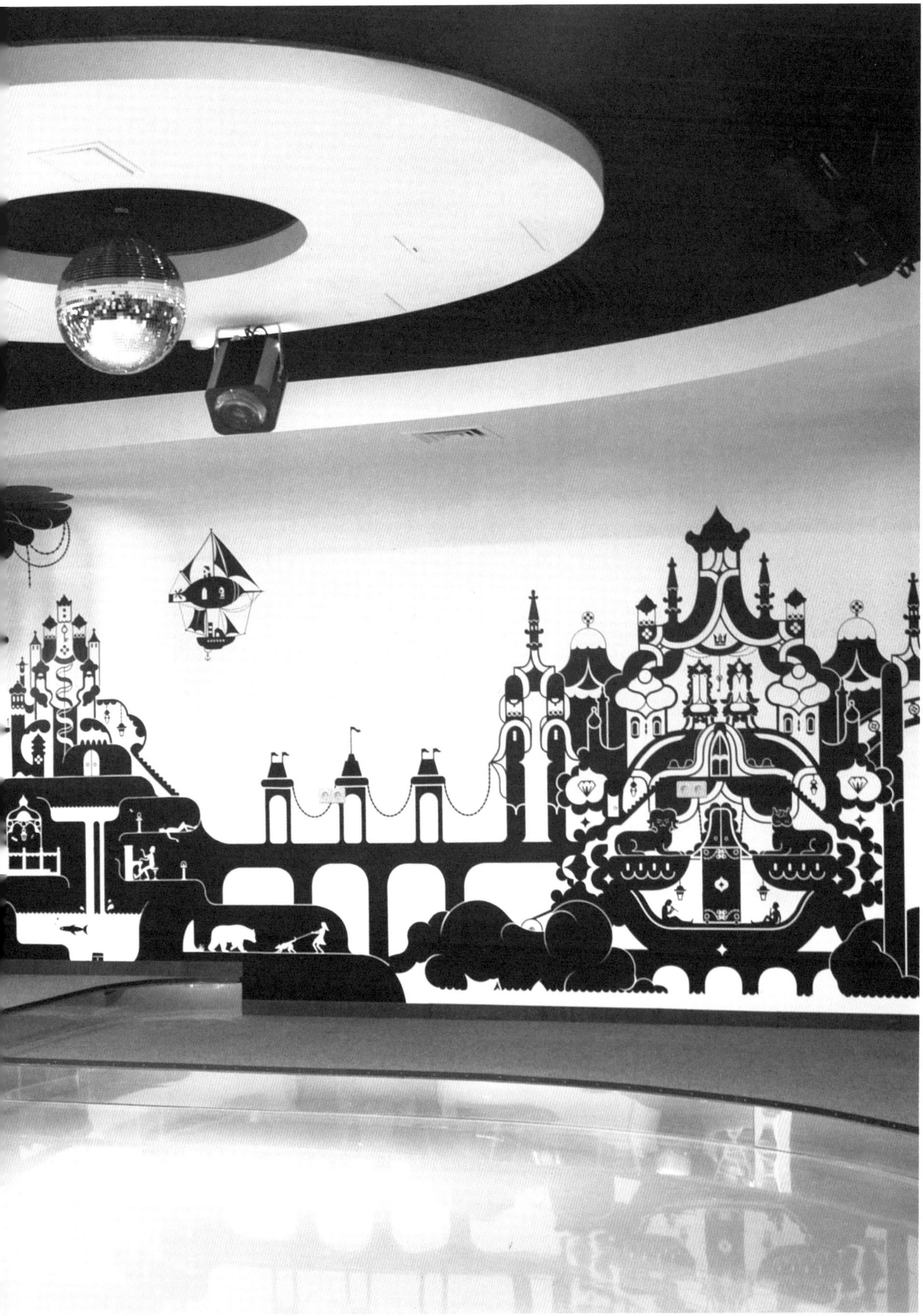

- Wall Art • Bar & Restaurant •

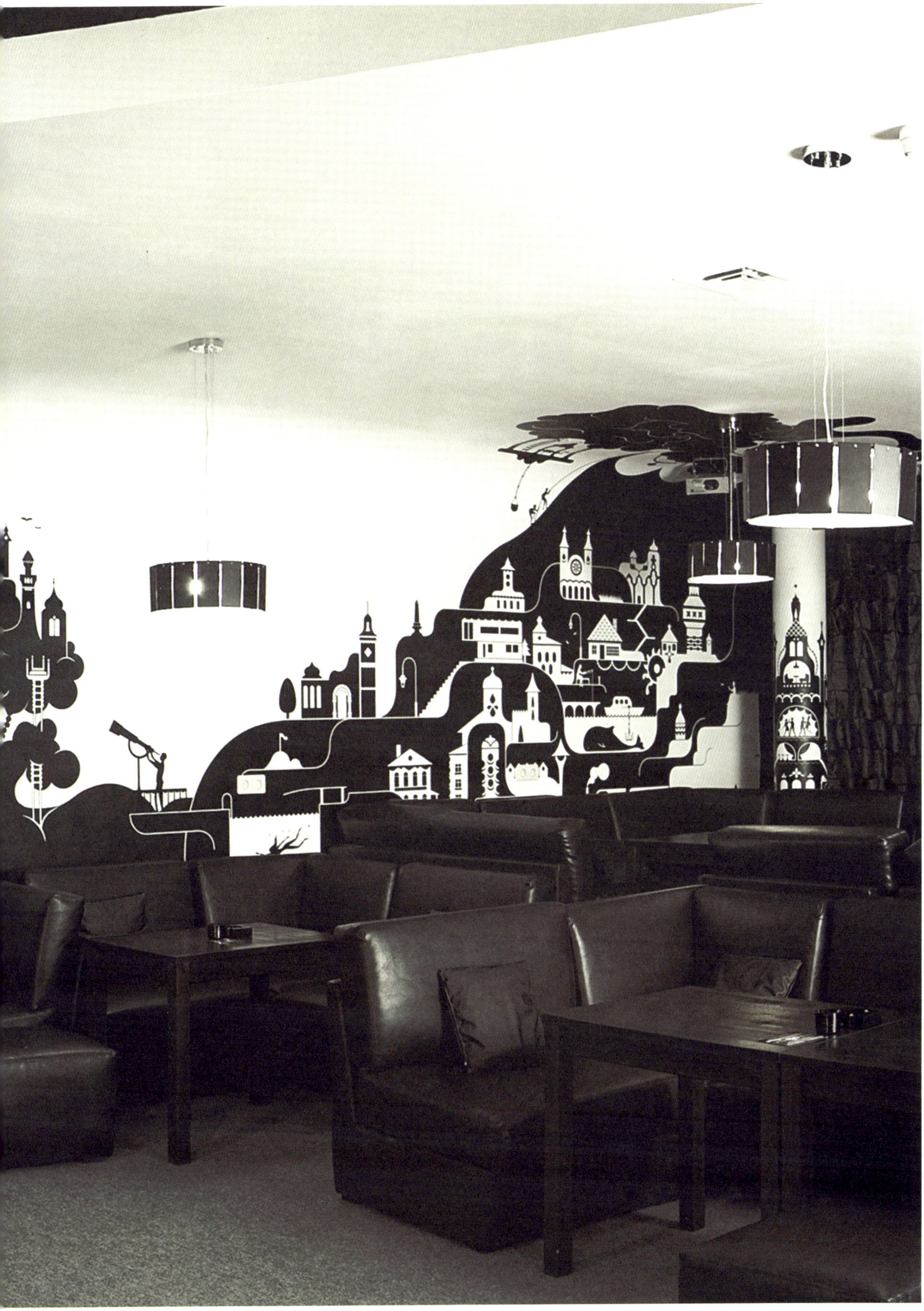

- Wall Art - Bar & Restaurant -

Wall-painting for Black Cat Bar

Completion Date: 2008
Design Firm: Bigpen Studio
Designer: Alexander Mikhaylov
Photographer: Alexander Mikhaylov
Client: Black Cat Bar

This wall-painting was conceived as a basic component of the small bar. Black Cat Bar has got a new owner who wanted to turn it into a meeting place for the youth, for small private music parties, where you can sit, have a couple of cocktails, or dance on a small dance floor.

The bar has 2 parts: the bar itself and the dance floor. The designers made the painting in black and white. The colour can be changed when changing the lighting from party to party.

The bar area is made in black, and the dancing one is white. Located on the tiles along the walls, the painting's feature is that it is drawn with little or no preliminary sketches. Some small sketches of a few parts are made, but the basic objects are drawn directly on the walls. The rest is pure imagination and improvisation.

This is a pleasant moment to design the wall, mainly due to the fact that the client let the designers to do with the wall anything they want.

Cristal Bar

Completion Date: 2008
Designer: Katrin Olina
Photographer: Katrin Olina ltd
Client: Cristal Bar

Cristal Bar, located on the ninth floor of a central Hong Kong high-rise, is an unexpected springboard to another dimension. The bar's interior is the latest project by Katrin Olina, the Icelandic designer and artist internationally acclaimed for her sleek graphic style, multilayered imagery, and unique stock of fantastical characters. At Cristal Bar, every wall, ceiling, and floor serves as a tableau in which Olina's signature forms dreamily swirl and collide. This immersive installation is neither like a backdrop, nor any other graphic design out there: Crossing into the realm of fine art, Olina's unparalleled work is like an explosion of scattered memories, an entire visual world that each viewer interprets in a profoundly personal way.

Inside Cristal Bar, the ambiance shifts subtly as the observer moves from point A to B. Glossy wall coverings spread seamlessly across every surface, yet morph in colour and pattern as they expand throughout the bar's four interconnected areas: The central space is awash with deep brown graphics depicting seaweed-like forms and hybrid water creatures that float by. In two adjacent rooms, the ceilings and surfaces are tinted vibrant red, alive with the winged silhouettes of ethereal cranes in flight. The third section—with turquoise-green walls and a panel of windows overlooking the street—is layered with graceful flowers and feathery forms, all to a light and lofty effect. Where these distinct areas meet, their differently colored graphics overlap in fluid transition. By distinguishing Cristal Bar's sections by décor (rather than doors), Olina creates several small environments that merge into one unified space.

BAR (the LOOP) 9th Floor / 33 Wellington Street, HK

Katrin Olina

www.katrin-olina.com
Drawing A7/3M film application
CEILING

DATE 18.05.08
ART WORK APPLICATION

94

95

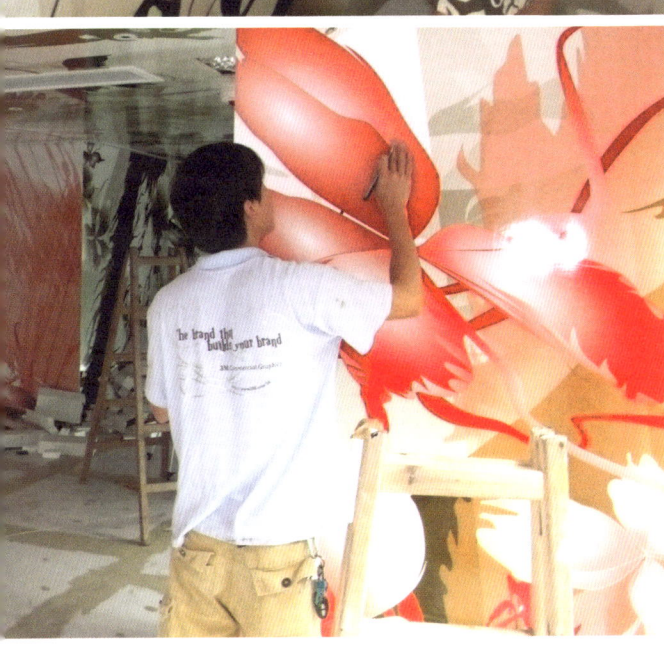

Teen Action

Completion Date: 2009
Design Firm: Estúdio Romeu & Julieta
Designer: Jean Campos
Photographer: Angelton
Client: Confrade

The cute wall-painting is created for the kids zone in the Confrade, Brazilian restaurant located in Cuiabá. Some interesting patterns in black and white well match the chairs in fresh green and make the room outstanding.

The painting is done with special pens for wall, by Jean Campos who is currently the head-artist of Estúdio Romeu & Julieta, a design team focuses on creating illustrations for various segments, especially advertising.

97

Café El Bache

Completion Date: 2009
Designer: Victor Sandoval
Photographer: Victor Sandova
Client: Café El Bache

The mural in a coffee shop near a high school was created in acrylic paints. In a colourful manner, the cartoonish representation of moons on the painting is smoking and drinking coffee, just having a good time.

The mural brings to life the entire place, being the centerpiece of the coffee shop.

La Voragine
Wine Bar

Completion Date: 2009
Designer: Victor Sandoval
Photographer: Victor Sandova
Client: La Voragine Wine Bar

An exterior decorative mural created on the streets of Mexico City just inches from the street where public transportation buses fly by. The image has nothing to do with any special theme, it's just a moon, a sun and a mask.

Café De La Flor Mural

Completion Date: 2010
Designer: Victor Sandoval
Photographer: Victor Sandova
Client: Café De La Flor

The mural covering an area of 6 X 25 feet depicts the freedom of flight and the colourful simplicity of birds. The background of the painting is different textile finishes which represents the different cultures and how they are all intertwined.

the interior of the café is an eclectic mix of mexican and arabic decorations, so a colourful mural is an excellent addition for creating a warm welcoming sense of belonging, the mural was created with acrylic paints, brushes, stencils and spray paint.

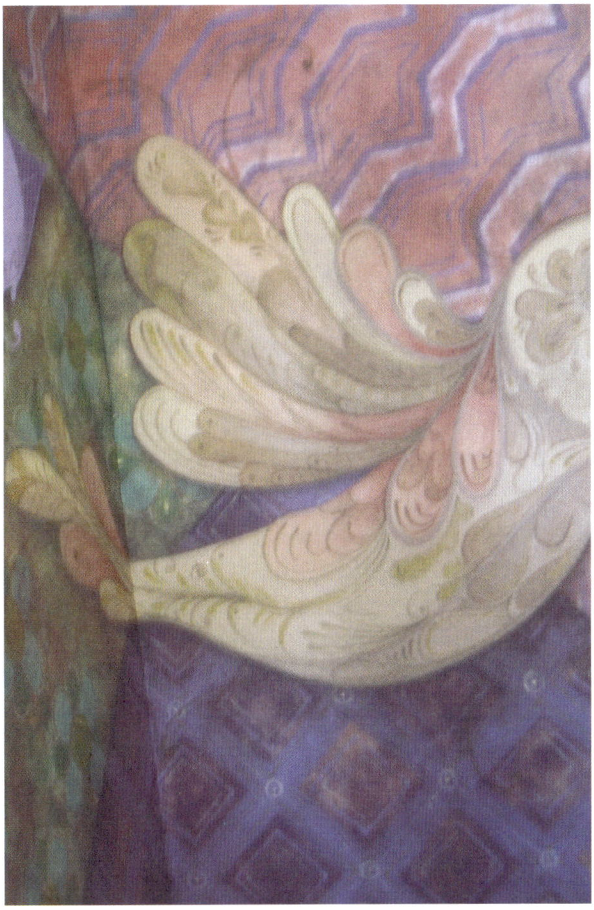

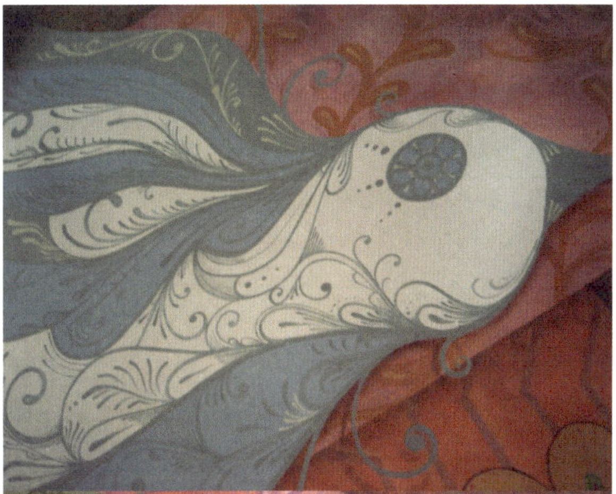

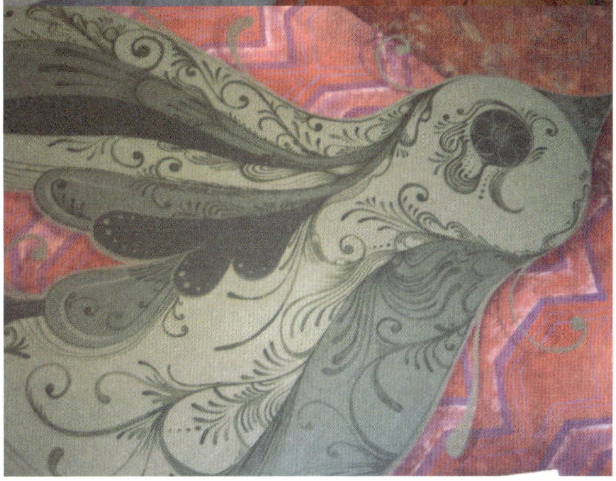

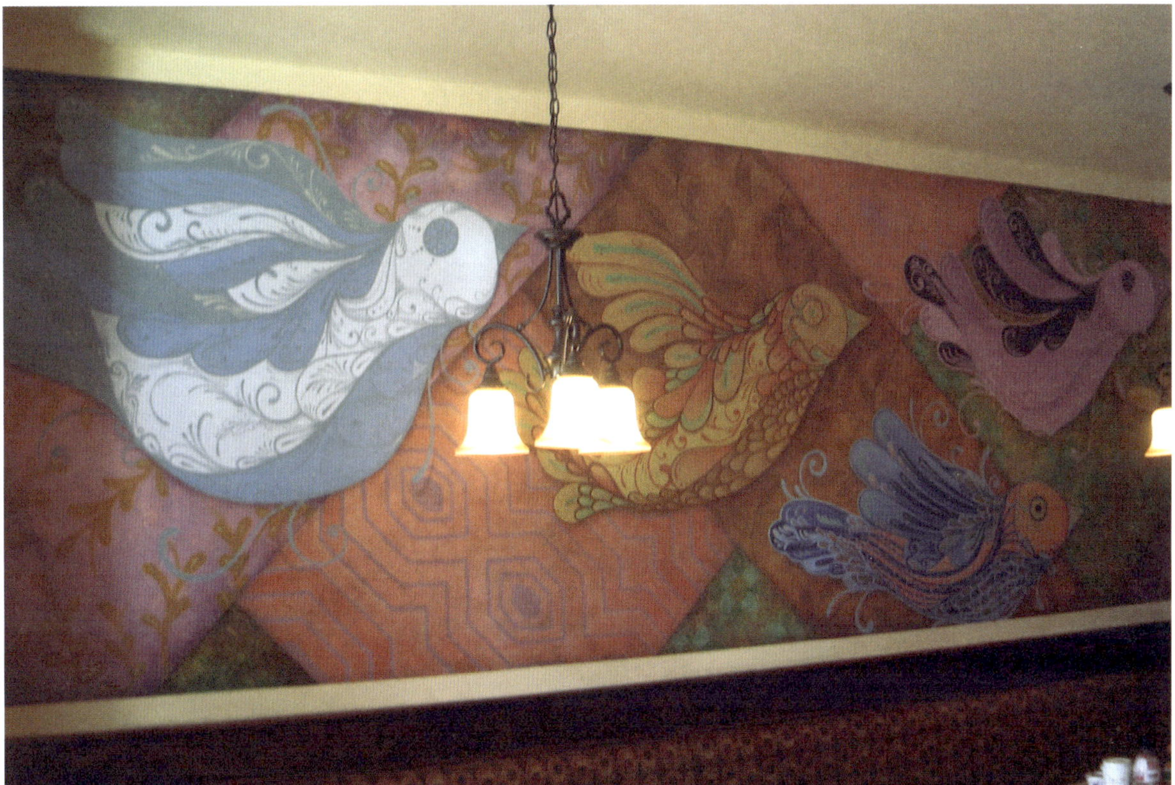

Australian Vine House

Completion Date: 2008
Design Firm: Art Group LAB261
Designers: KFKS, SFHD
Photographer: SFHD, Anna Novikova
Client: Australian Vine House Restaurant, Russia

The interior walls in Australian Wine House Restaurant were decorated with graphics in the style of ancient tribal art of Australian continent.

The graphics were created with a sense of dynamics, laconic expressiveness stroke, specificity in the transmission of motion. Monochrome, thin lines, Australians depict people are always in motion.

Performed within a week, the whole work include the design of entrance, bar, decorated room and entrance in toilets. During the implementation the white oil paint (markers) was adopted to decorate the walls.

103

- Wall Art • Bar & Restaurant •

104

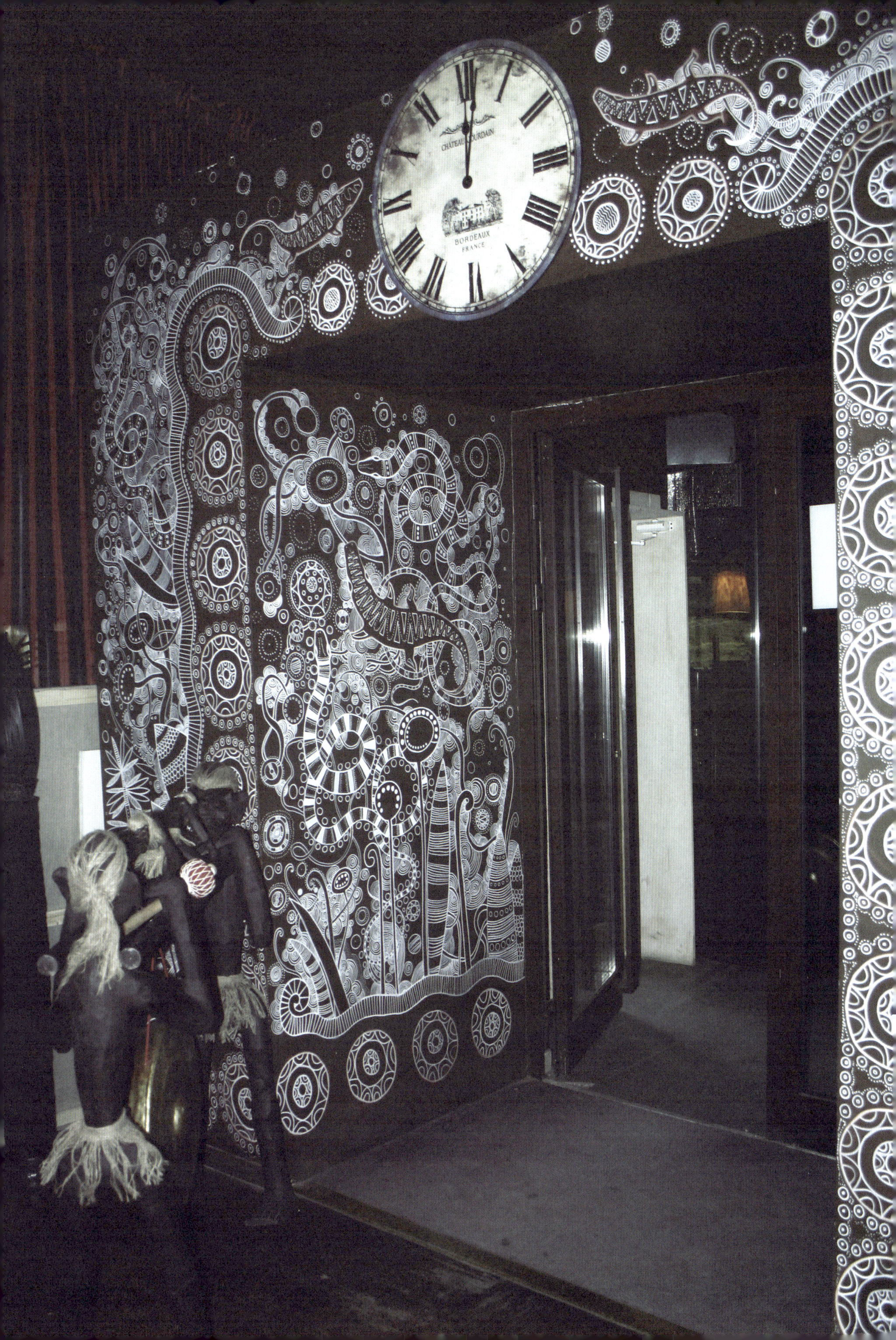
BORDEAUX
FRANCE

Energy 2000

Completion Date: 2008
Design Firm: Nawer Artde7 & Archipro
Photographer: Nawer
Client: Energy 2000

Energy 2000 music club is one of the largest and most contemporary clubs in Poland. The interior design project came into being parallel with the painting of the wall mounted graphics, which provided inspiration for the creation of lighting, tables, box seating and bars.

The harmonic continuity between the painted graphics and architecture along with the innovative use of RGB LED lighting emphasizes the futuristic design in the comfortable space.

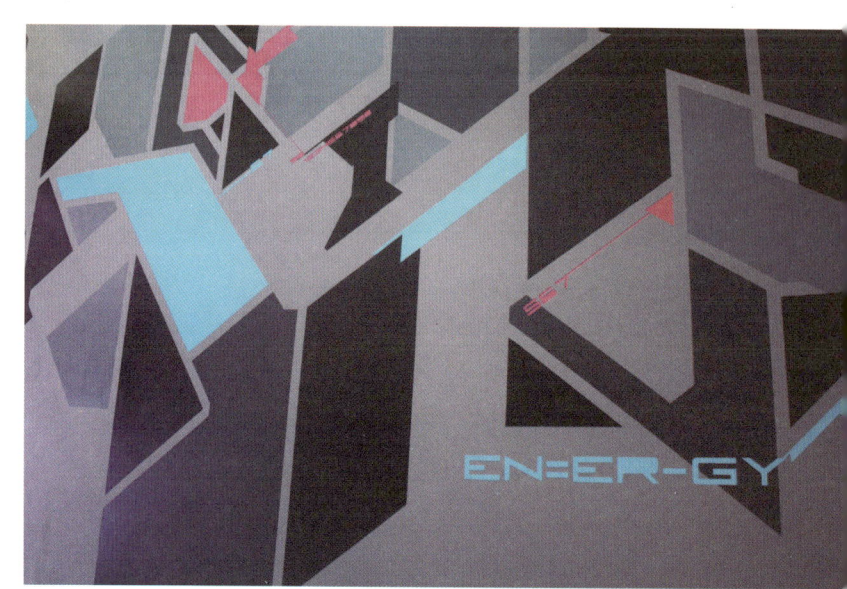

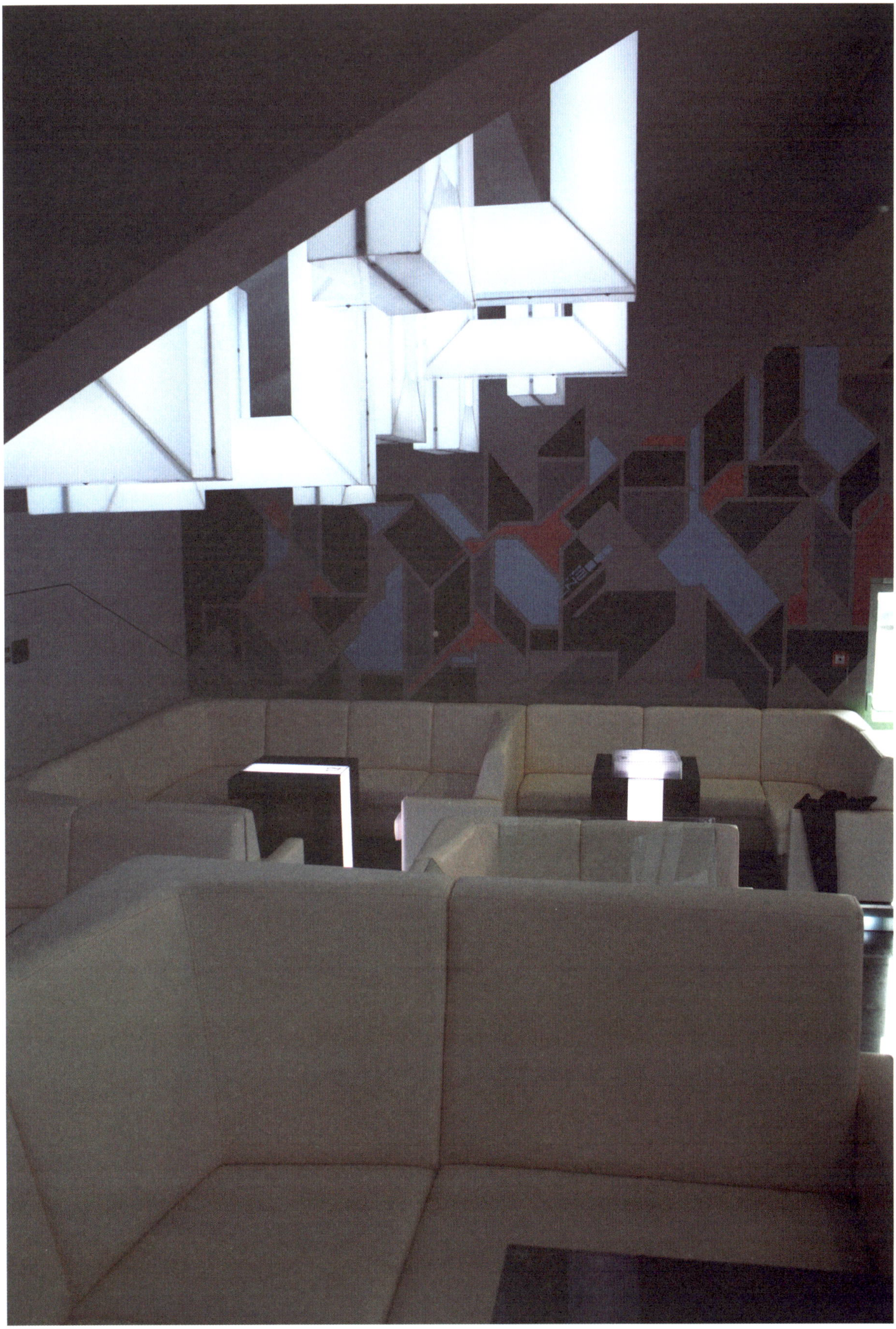

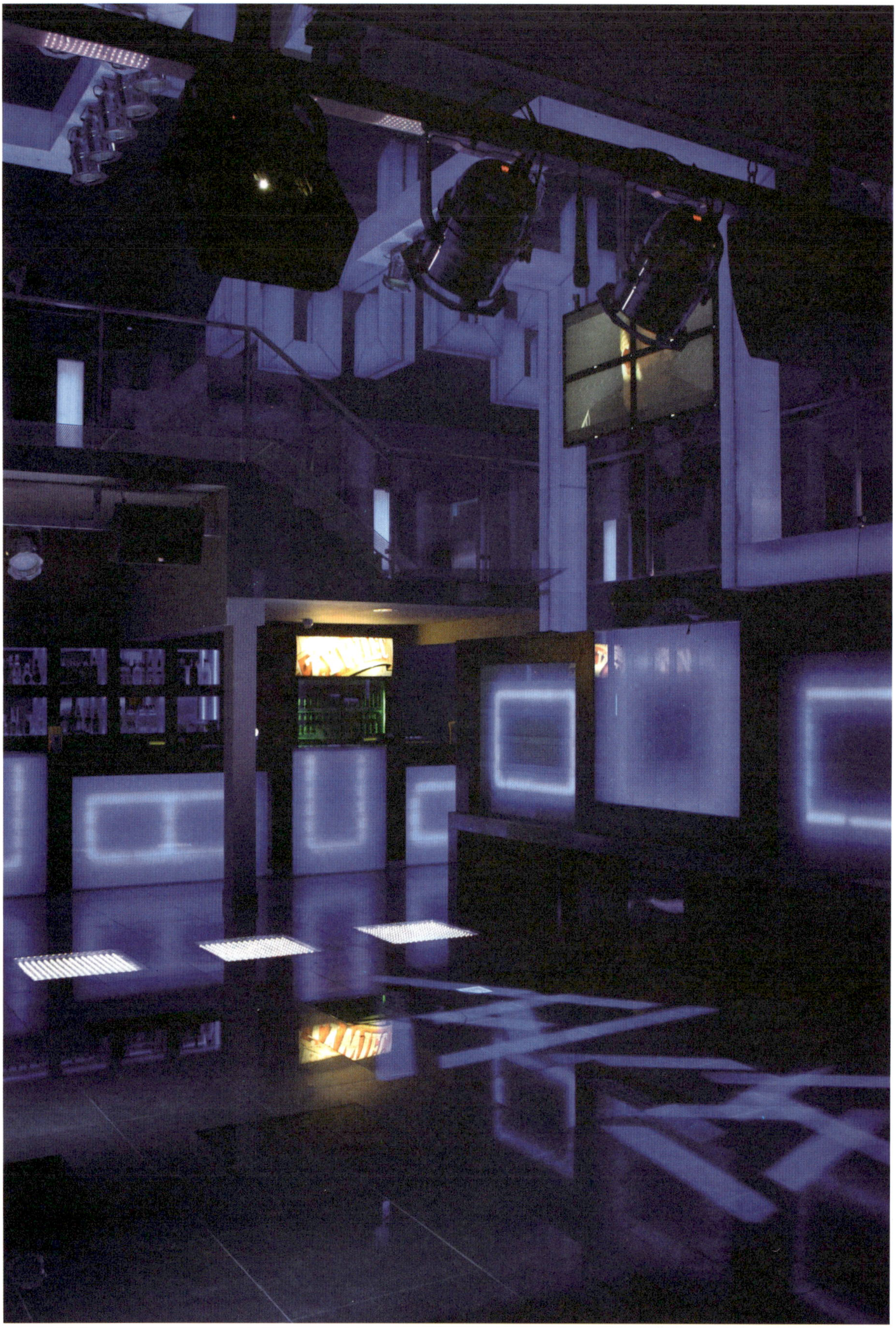

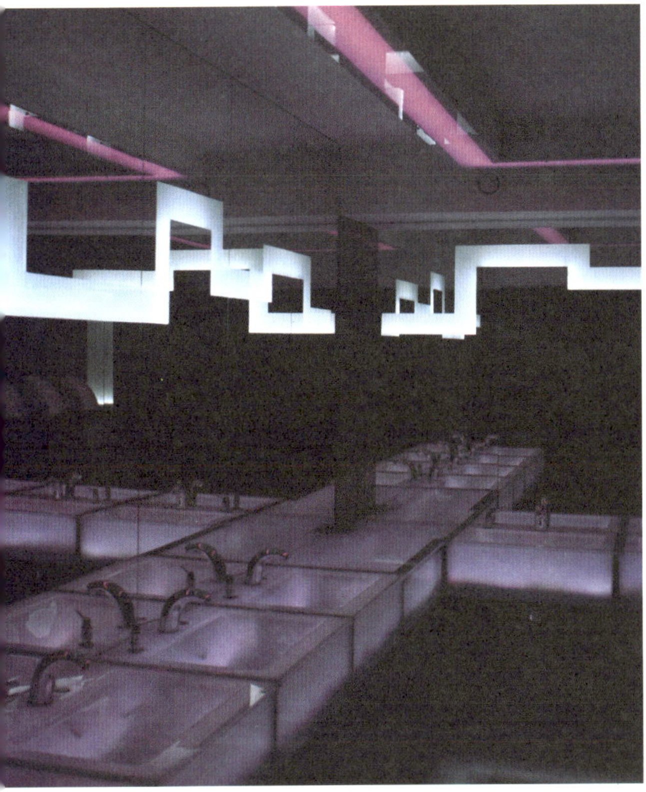
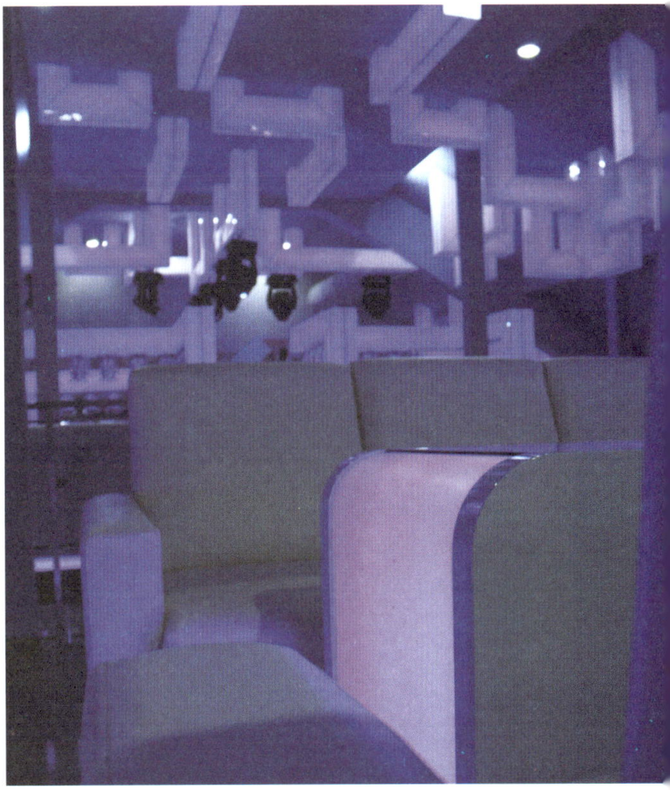
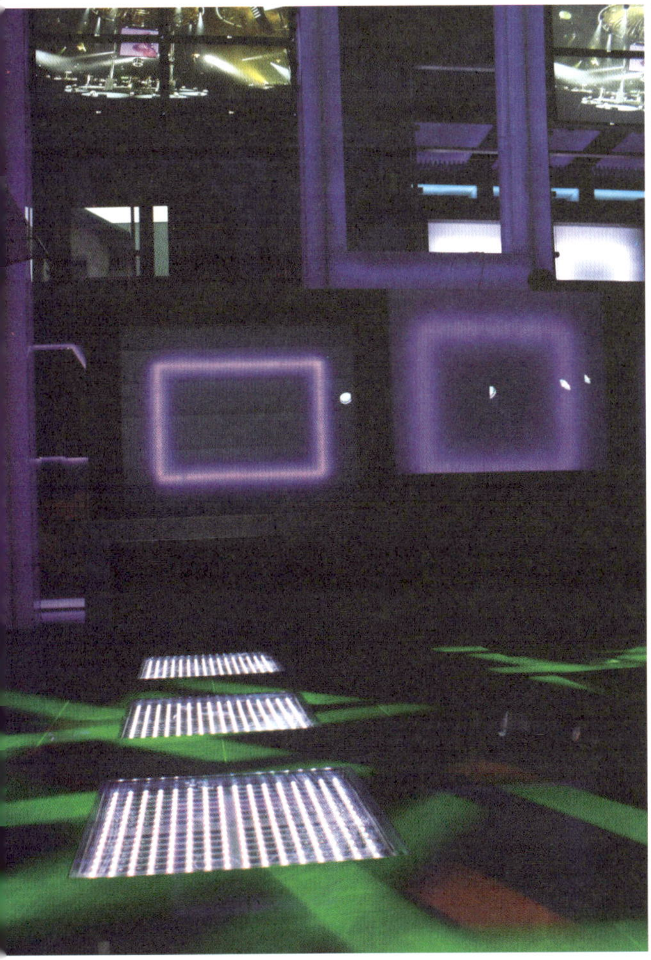
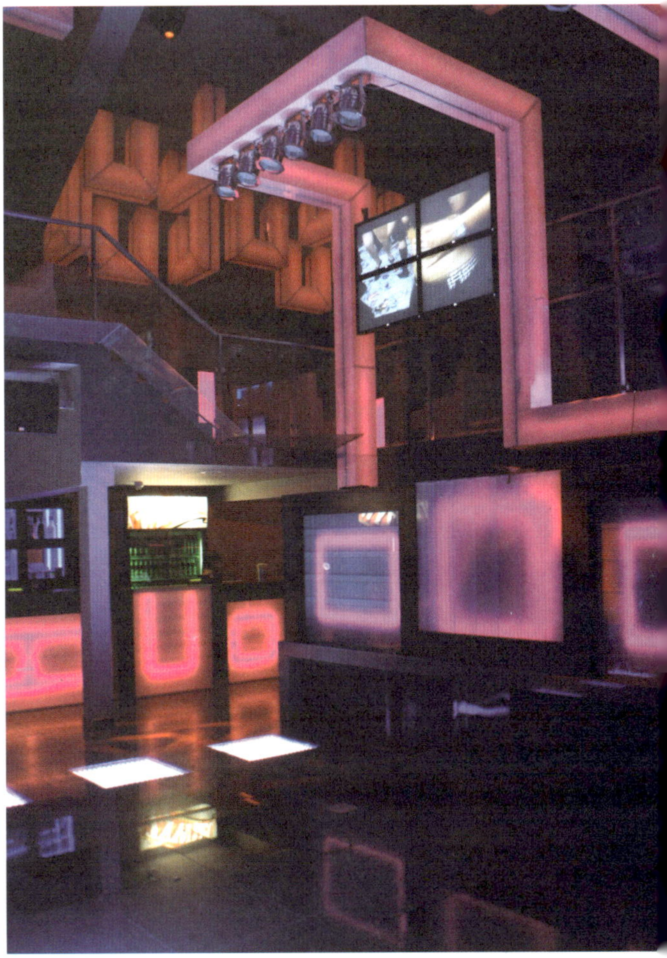

Offside Interior

Completion Date: 2010
Design Firm: Neosbrand
Art Director & Creative: Fidel Castro
Illustration: Susana Castillo
Strategic Planner: Javier Castro

This is an illustration and graphic design for the interior of a new Club. As a recreation of different world, with the aim of representing only a dream, the abstract work provides a differential value and elegant atmosphere for the cool club.

The graphics featured on the walls and floors are full of free and flowing feelings, and some details of the illusion and the lovely colours fully reflect the designers' talent and the whole work's wonderful concept.

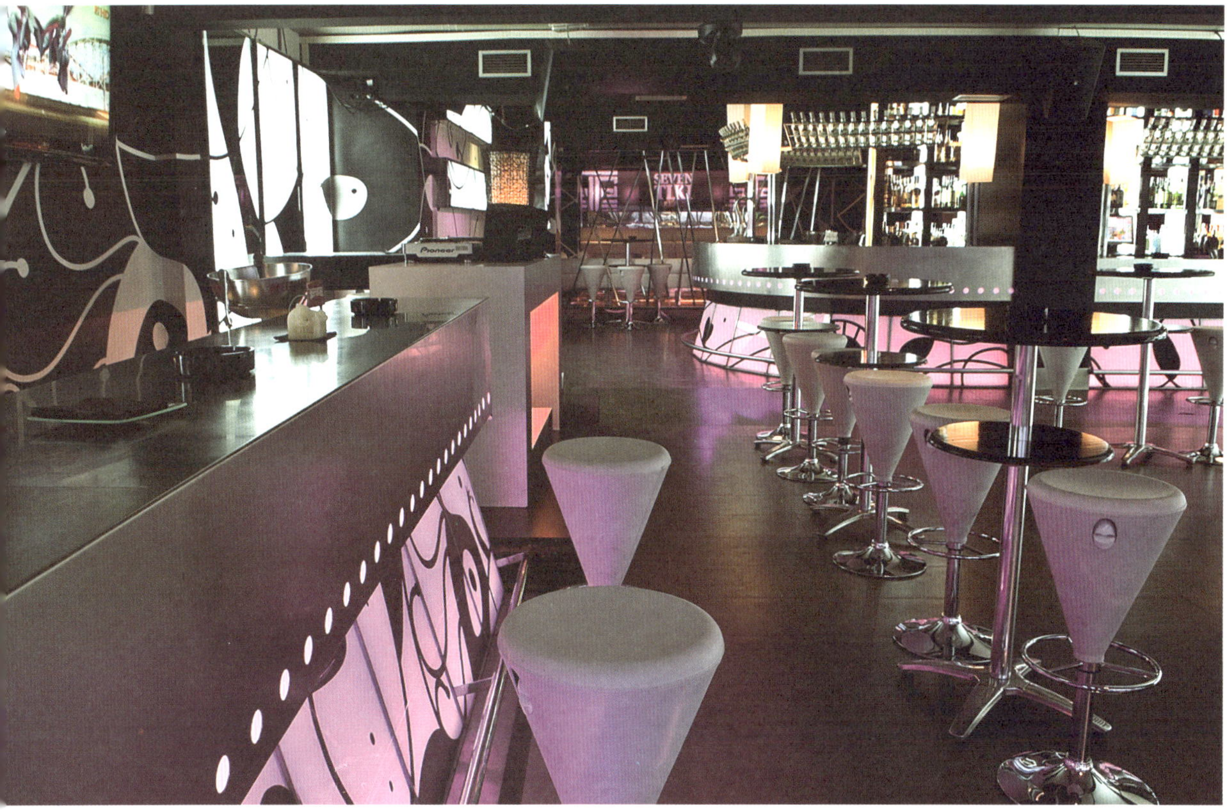
Pioneer

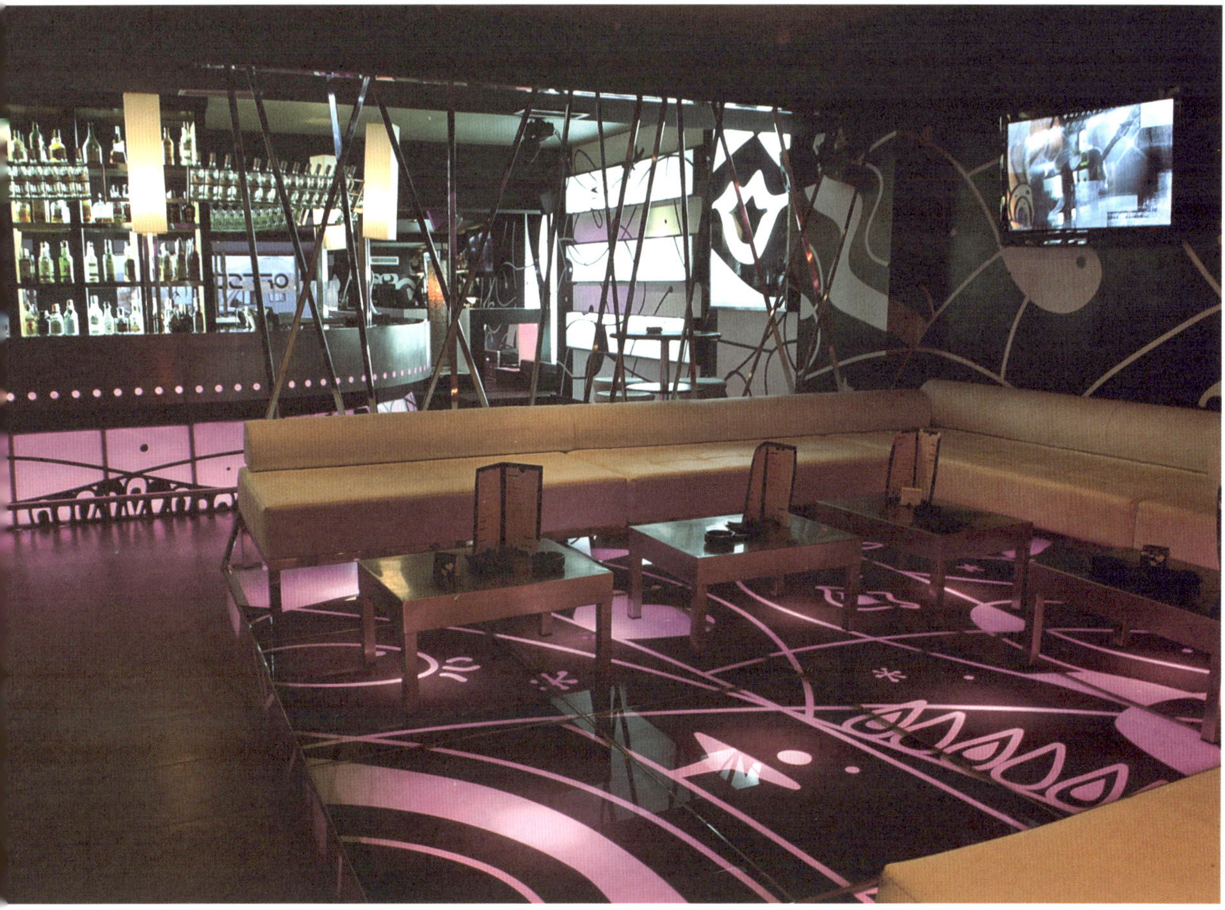

Wall Art • Bar & Restaurant •

113

Berry Hill "Uth" Center

Completion Date: 2009
Design Firm: LeighLeigh
Photographer: Chris Denner
Client: Innersmile / Stoke-On-Trent Council

Stoke city council commissioned Innersmile to "kit-out" 11 of their youth centers, Berry Hill is the fourth of these youth centers to be given the innersmile treatment. The project was held together using some of Luke Kirbalija's superbly crafted space themed graphics and photoshop work. LeighLeigh's contribution lays within the main beam signage, and a large scale illustration themes upon the future and alien space, creating hand puppets in a surreal vector environment.

- Wall Art
- Bar & Restaurant

115

Canvas Bar

Completion Date: 2010
Design Firm: Alexa Nice Interior Design
Photographer: Jonathan Baginski
Client: Marco & Emily Nunes,
Bonnie Shearston & Tom Sanceau

Canvas cocktail/wine bar brings a taste of small bar culture to Brisbane offering cocktails expertly mixed by internationally awarded mixologists, boutique wine, craft beer and a selection of 'design your own' food boards and tapas.

Take a front row seat at the white onyx bar to watch bartenders carve ice directly from an ice block and concoct their own homemade bitters, or sink into one of the lounges and sample a drinks menu ranging from shared punch bowls to absinthe fountains, Canvas twists on cocktail classics and more modern creations. Designer, Alexa Nice's main objective was to provide an intimate, warm and comfortable interior, utilising the quite small and narrow shell.

Renowned for her decadent design style, and detailed interior works, Nice truly pieced, the opulent booth seating, upholstered in luxurious velvets, leathers and silks, and an eclectic mix of modern and vintage furniture carefully together. The rich recycled timber paneling and planter boxes are beautifully highlighted against the feature custom art work on the walls, by Jimmy Bligs and Troy James. The exposed incandescent light bulbs bring to light the raw beauty of the recycled timbers, and they are a contrasting element to the vintage feel.

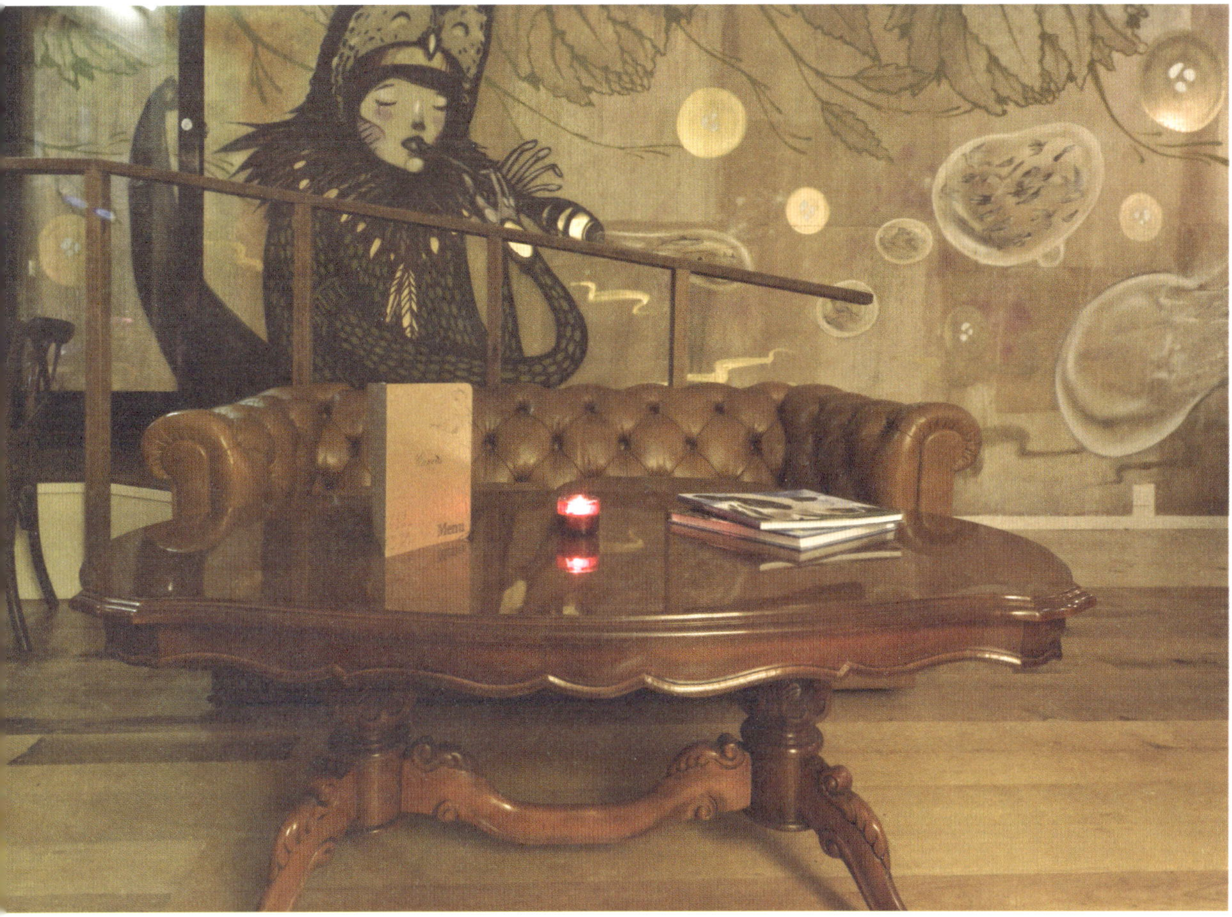
Menu

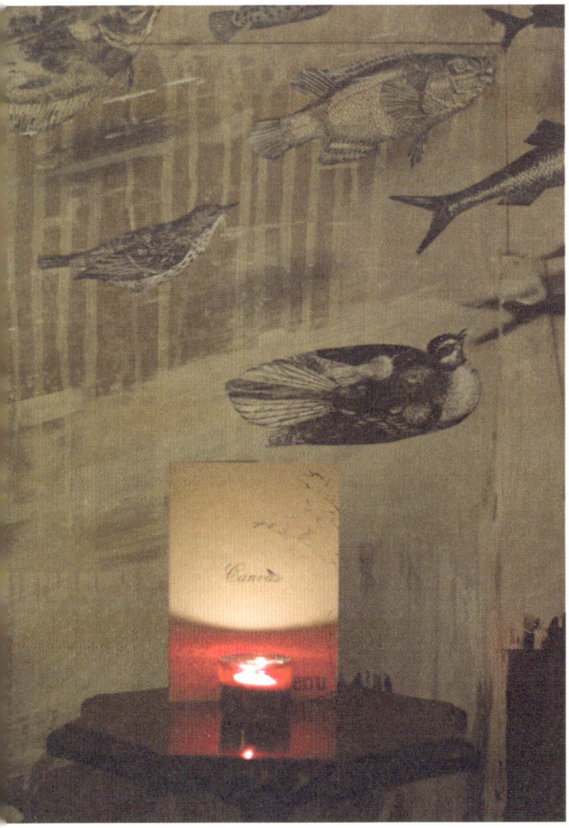
Canvas

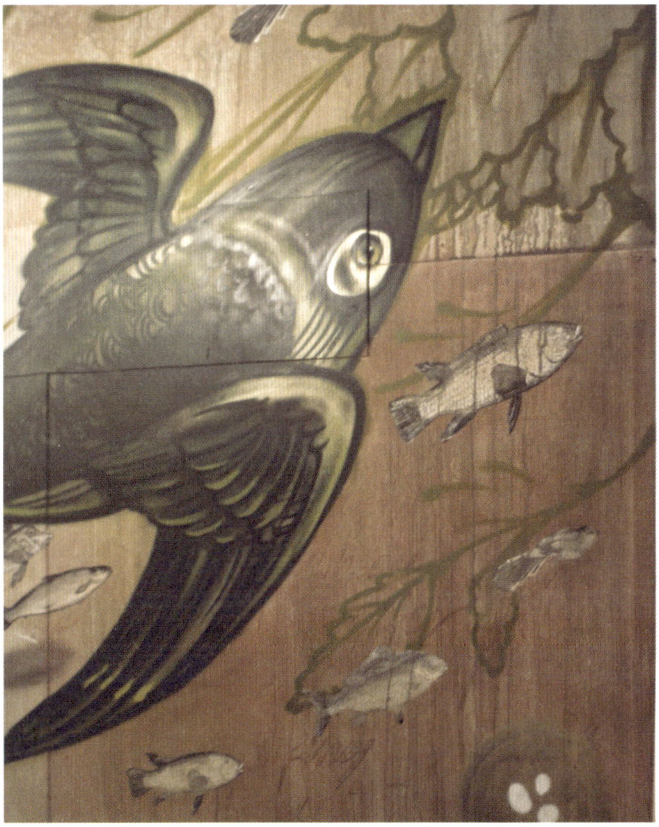

Dynamic curves
Geometric
Natural
a+b>c=ac+bc
2x²+3y²
27x6=162
12+4
How to drive this tricycle ds far as possible!
small strong warm faster

Wall Art • Exhibit

Fun-occult

Completion Date: February 2010
Designer: Good Wives and Warriors
Photographer: Good Wives and Warriors
Client: Recoat Gallery, Glasgow

"Fun-occult" exhibition designed at the Recoat Gallery combined drawings, wall-paintings and window drawings together, exploring the aesthetic symbols of pseudo-science and religion using a playful and light-hearted approach.

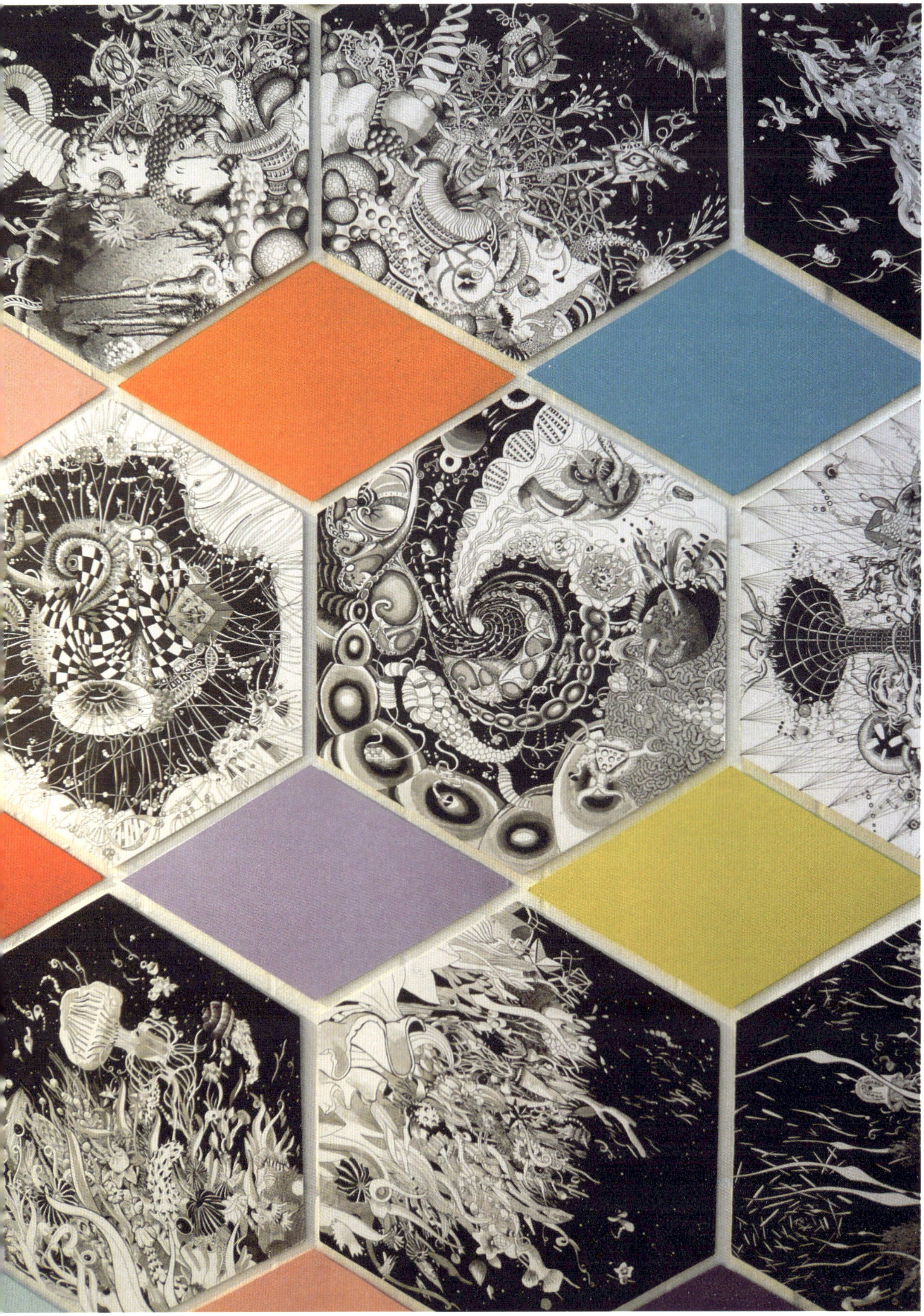

Buckminster-Fullerene Dream

Completion Date: January 2010
Designers: Good Wives and Warriors
Photographer: Venetia Van Hoorn Alkema
Client: Space In Between Pop-up Gallery, London, UK

Buckminsterfullerene Dream is an exhibition of wall-paintings, floor paintings and 3D drawing sculptures based on the "origin of life" theories.

Ranging from the quaint to the curious, the absurd to the plausible, the work refers directly to the "Origin of Life" theories, but from a Wikipedia knowledge stand point. The paintings were created directly onto the walls and floor in a pop-up gallery space in Clerkenwell, London.

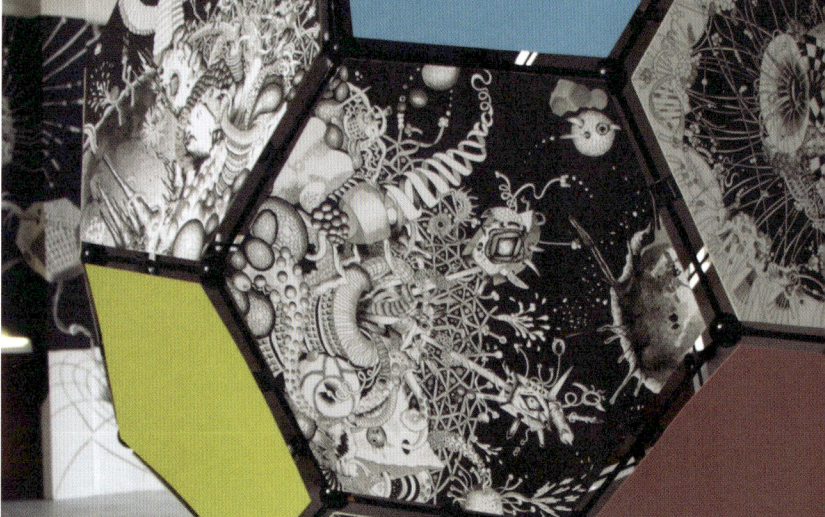

123

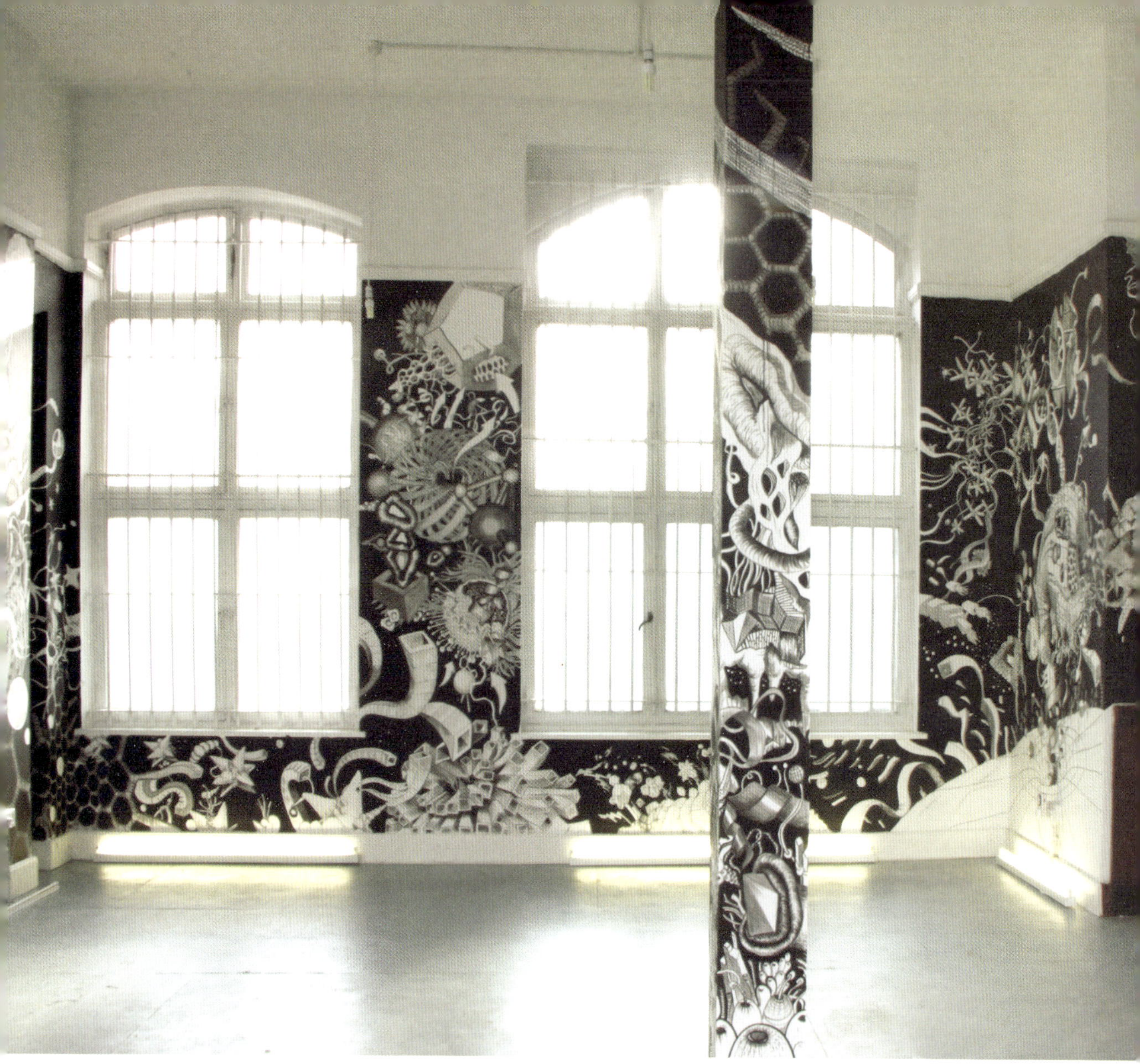

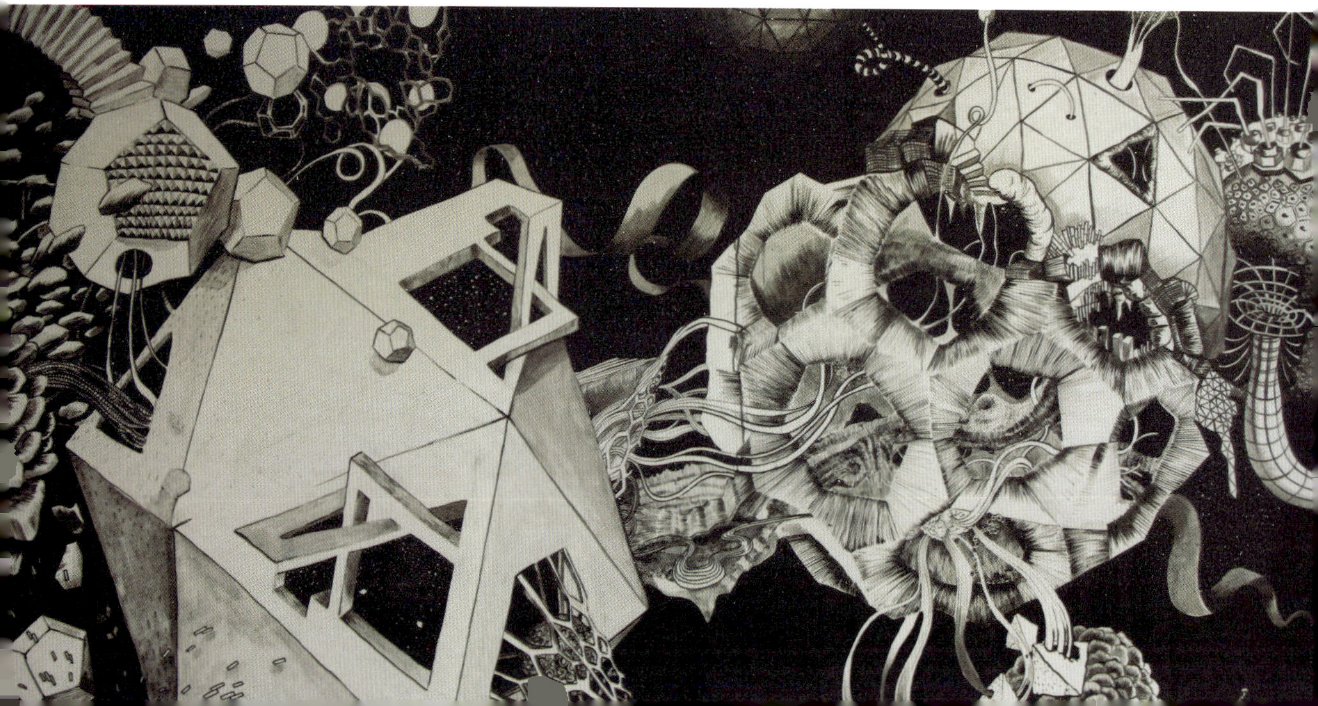

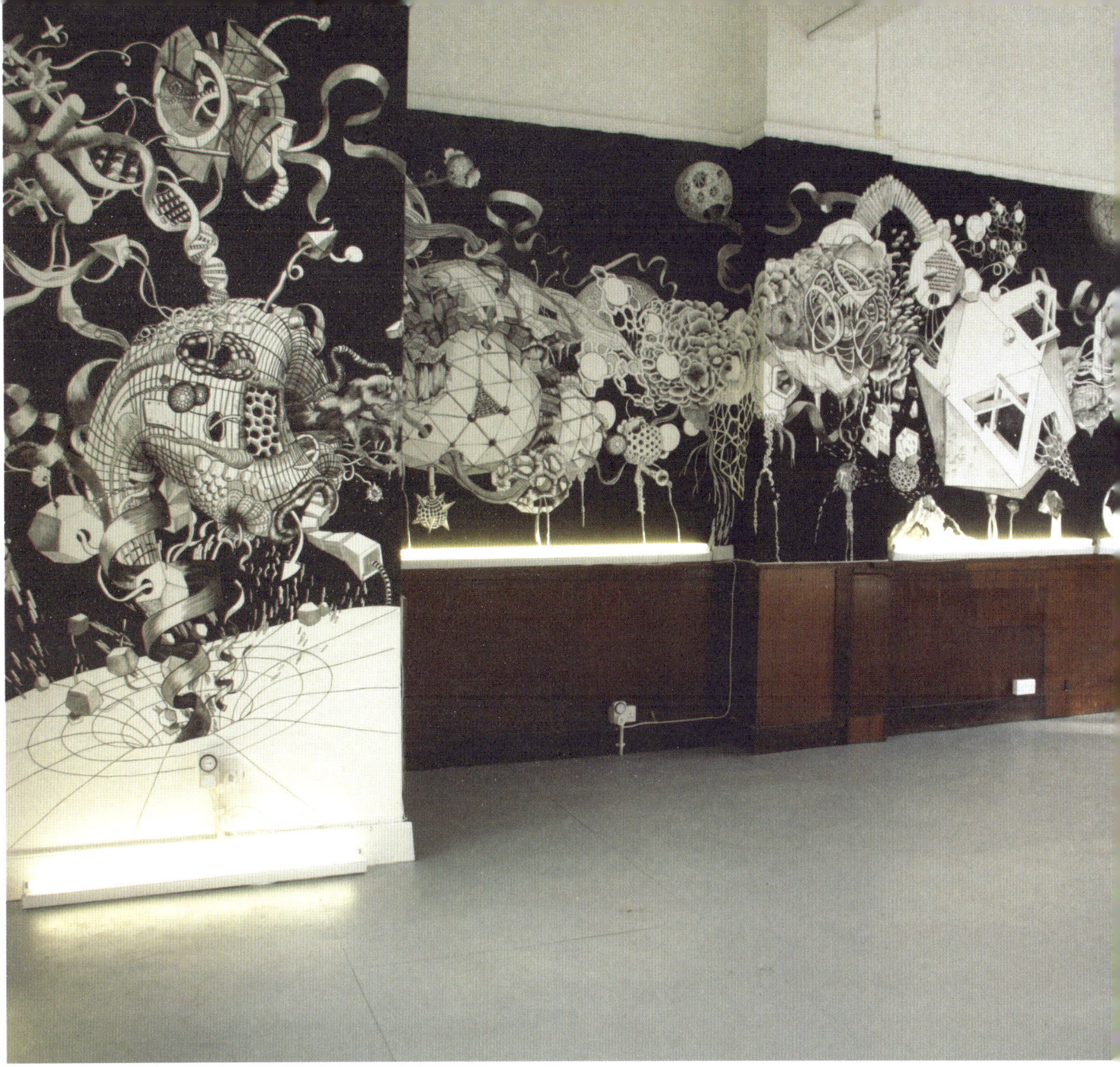

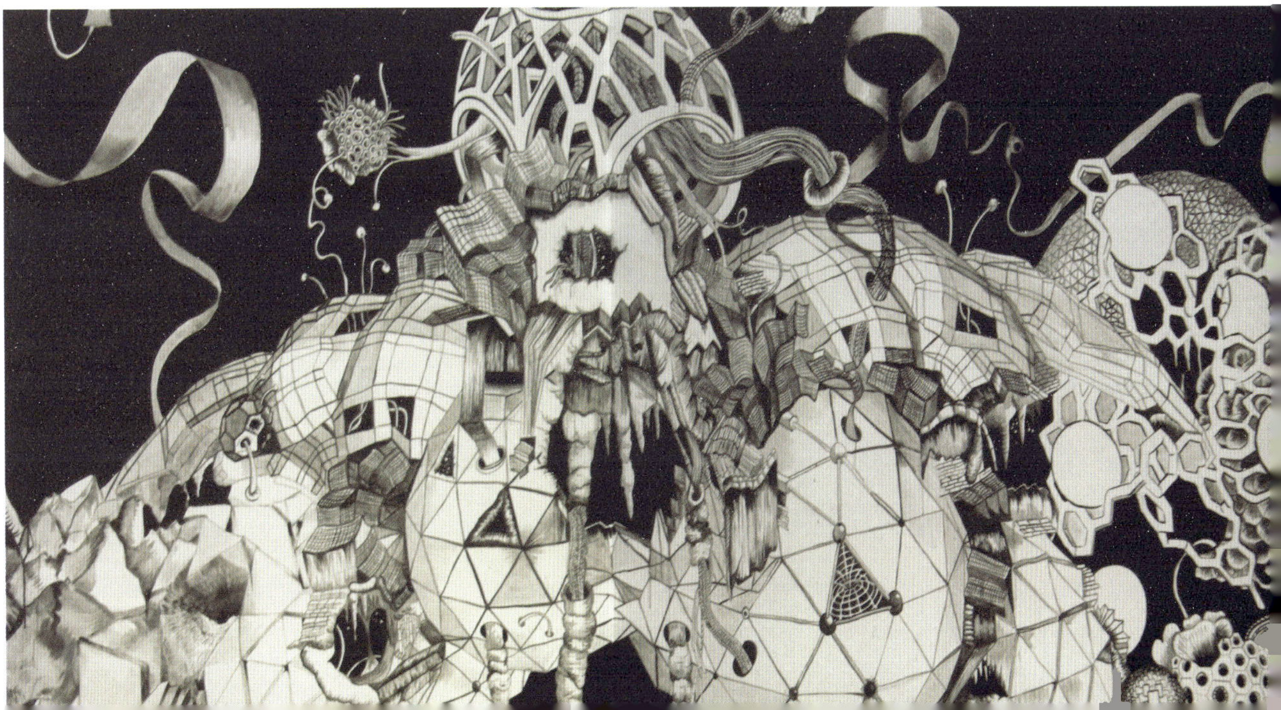

Art of Persuading Exhibition Entrance Room

Completion Date: 2007
Designer: Branimir Sabljić
Photographers: Damir Fabijani, Branimir Sabljić
Client: Studio Rašić

"Graffiti Room" is the introduction to the exhibition Art of Persuading which was organized by the Croatian Advertising Association and the Museum of Arts and Crafts in Zagreb for celebrating 170 years of advertising in Croatia.

The space graphically illustrates the five sections of the exhibition: 1) target groups, 2) method/communication channels, 3) messages/meanings, 4) media and 5) advertising politics and policy. All the outstanding graphic works for the wall decoration left a deep impression on the visitors.

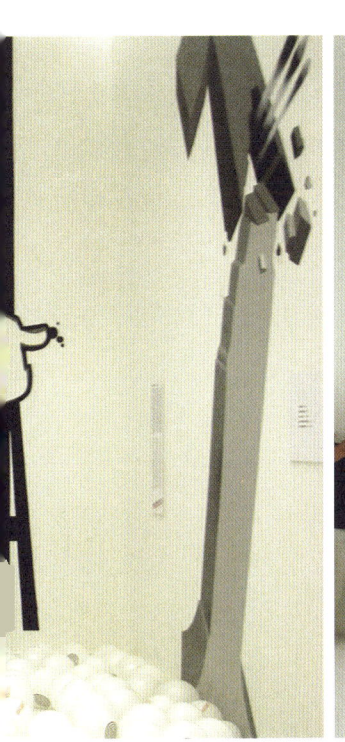

CILJANE SK
target groups

MED
medium

PORUKE / ZNAČENJA
messages / significations

MEDIJI
medium

- Wall Art
- Exhibit

Exhibition Design
Torture Basement

Completion Date: 2010
Designers: Trapped in Suburbia
Client: Museum Gouda

Trapped in Suburbia was asked to redesign the torture exhibition in the cellar of Museum Gouda. Before the designing, the designers considered how to make it more exciting and get kids to read the little signs next to the torture equipment. They decided to make it an experience by putting all the information on the floor with UV-paint finally. In this way the visitors can only see something when they put on the UV-flash light otherwise it is just a white floor. All the info on the floor is hand drawn, even the text. It is really exciting work from which you can explore and discover unexpected things.

129

- Wall Art
- Exhibit

Welkom in de Martelkelder!

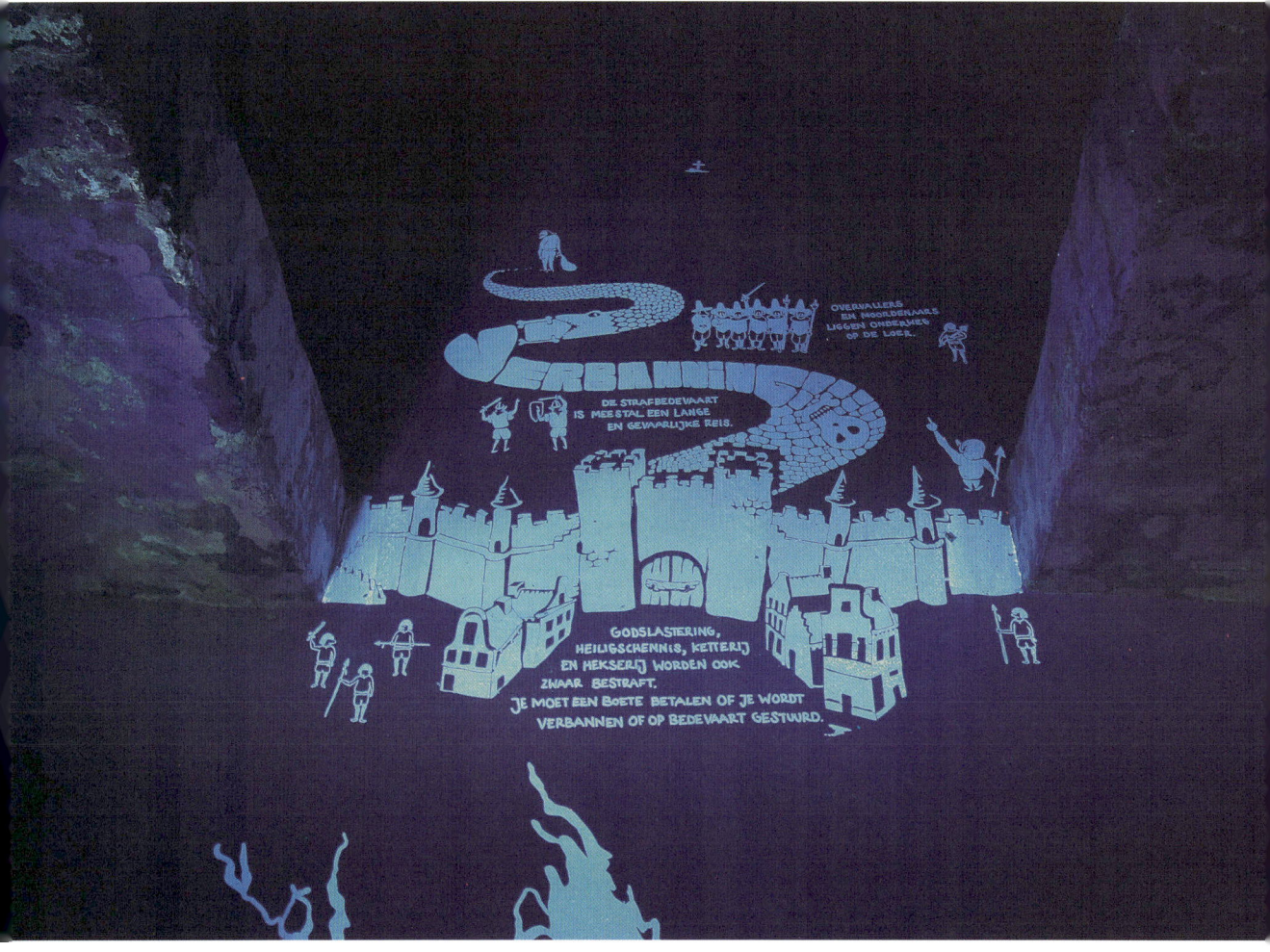

IJzeren Pijn

Verbanning

De strafbedevaart is meestal een lange en gevaarlijke reis.

Overvallers en moordenaars liggen onderweg op de loer.

Godslastering, heiligschennis, ketterij en hekserij worden ook zwaar bestraft. Je moet een boete betalen of je wordt verbannen of op bedevaart gestuurd.

Vuurhaard

Stadsgalg

De stadsgalg staat meestal op een plek in de stad waar iedereen hem goed kan zien. De lichamen van de misdadigers hangen zo mogelijk aan de galg als waarschuwing voor voorbijgangers.

Het is een teken dat de wet hier serieus genomen moet worden.

Aan deze stadsgalg kunnen vier veroordeelden tegelijk worden opgehangen.

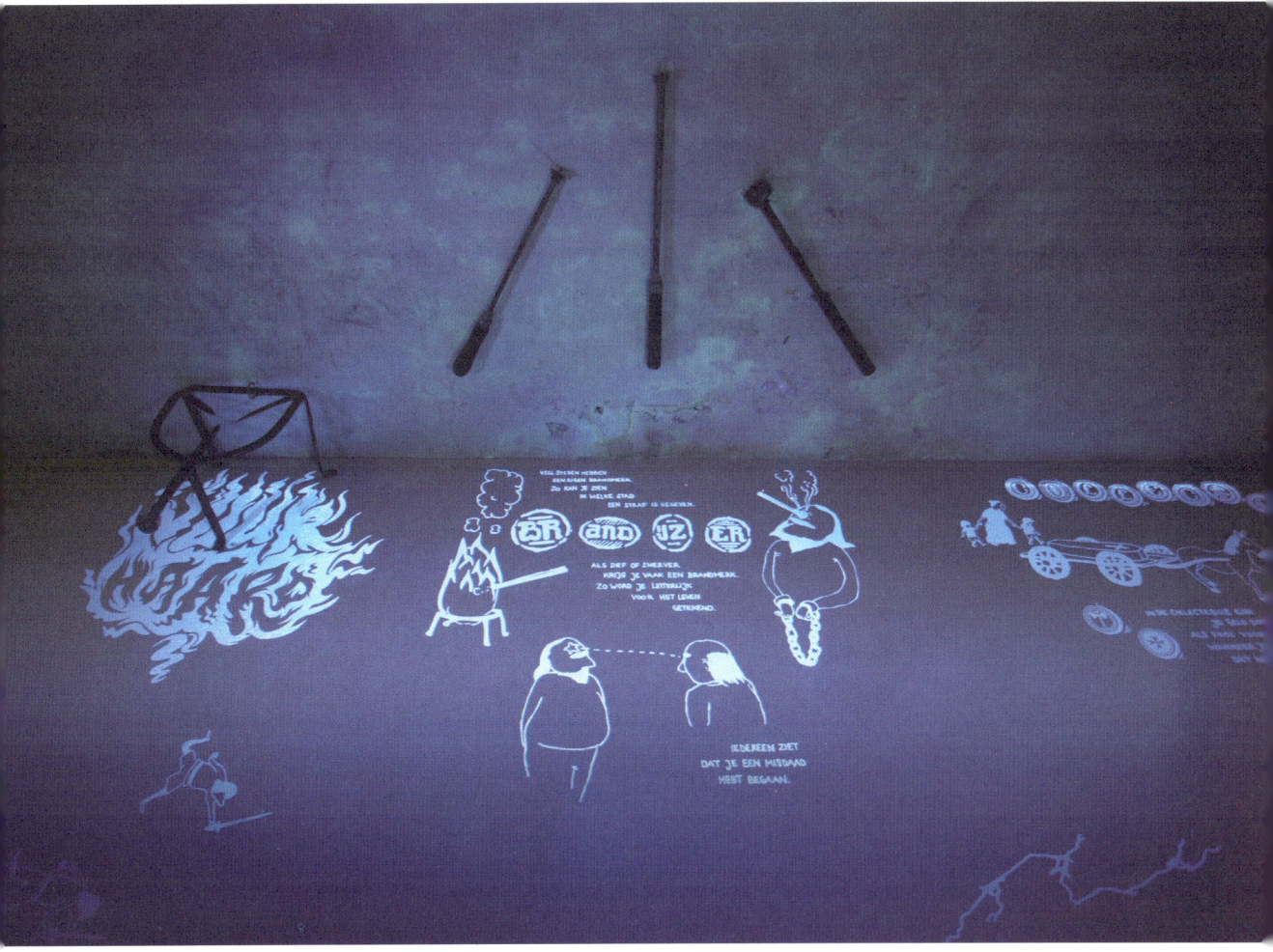

Veel steden hebben een eigen brandmerk. Zo kan je zien in welke stad een straf is gegeven.

Als dief of zwerver krijg je vaak een brandmerk. Zo word je letterlijk voor het leven getekend.

Iedereen ziet dat je een misdaad hebt begaan.

Reykjavik Art Museum

Completion Date: 2008
Designer: Katrin Olina
Photographer: Katrin Olina ltd
Client: Reykjavik Art Museum

This is a large-scale installation created by Olina titled Eulenspiegel debuted at the Reykjavik Museum in Iceland. The installation is part of "ID Lab," a much-anticipated exhibition showcasing works by other important Icelandic artists including Hrafnildur Arnardóttir (a.k.a. Shoplifter) and collaborative group The Icelandic Love Corporation.

As her presence in the Visual Art world becomes increasingly prominent, Katrin Olina's work, though graphic in nature, cannot be pigeonholed solely into the realm of design. The 85-square-meter installation – spanning across the walls and floor – is accompanied by an animation piece: at one end of the installation, a circular "white hole" projection depicts a swirling, creative source ejecting Olina's imagery; at the other end is an animated "black hole" tunnel that absorbs these visual elements back in again. In between, Olina's fixed wall illustrations take on a dynamic narrative. Olina worked on the animation with Caoz in Iceland and musician Gisli Galdur.

In the Reykjavik Museum show, Olina's otherworldly graphics fusing to the walls thanks to specialized films fashioned by material manufacturer 3M.

- Wall Art
- Exhibit

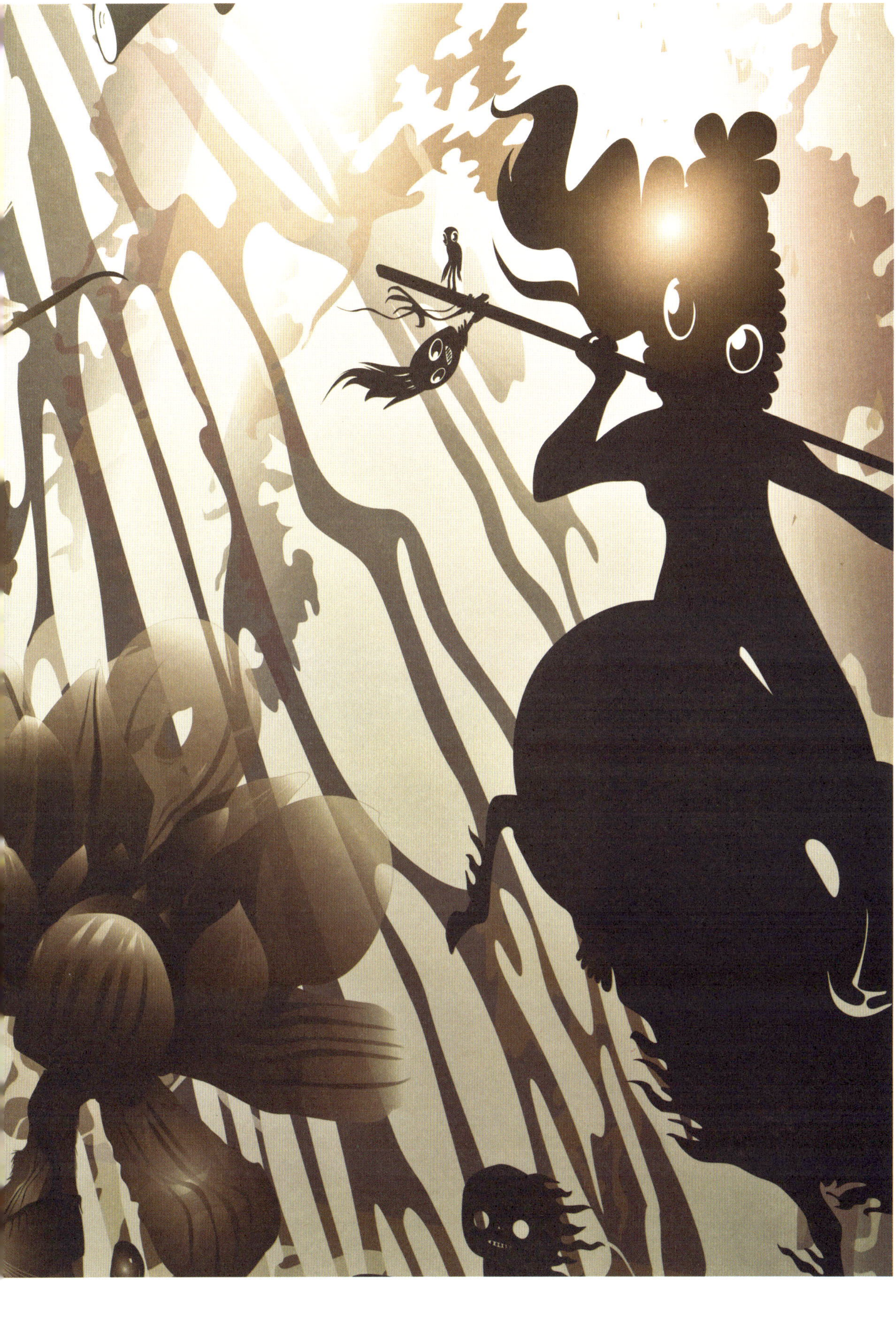

- Wall Art
- Exhibit

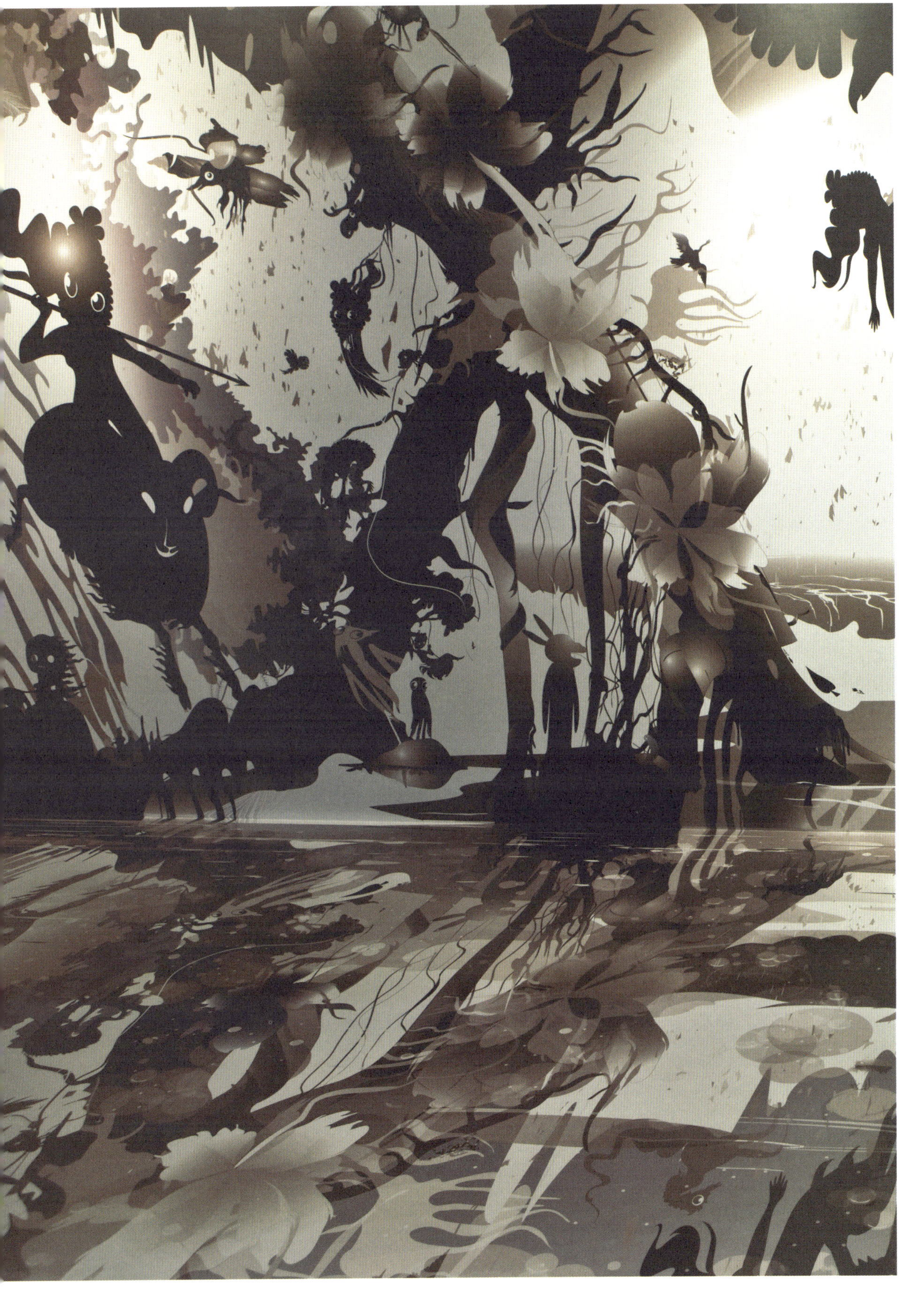

• Wall Art • Exhibit •

Matisse &

Completion Date: 2005
Designers: Malene Landgreen
Photographer: Anders Sune Berg
Client: Statens Kunstmuseum, Copenhagen, Denmark

As Malene Landgreen's other works, this one designed for museum interiors derives meaning from the fact that the uncertain, abstract, unformulated, chaotic and inharmonious, no less than the well-ordered, well-considered and flawless, always relates proportionally to something else.

No matter how incomprehensible and ungraspable it might be, indeed precisely because it is. It's all about relations and proportions. That applies in art, architecture and life. Proportions are crucial, those in the mind as well as those in the surroundings where, as visual or mental presence, they establish harmonies and coherence of which thoughts and feelings are component parts. Proportions are specific and identifiable. They define time and space.

Arena Wall-painting

Completion Date: 2008
Designer: Malene Landgreen
Photographer: Anders Sune Berg
Client: Aarhus Kunstbygning,
Denmark, Copenhagen, Denmark

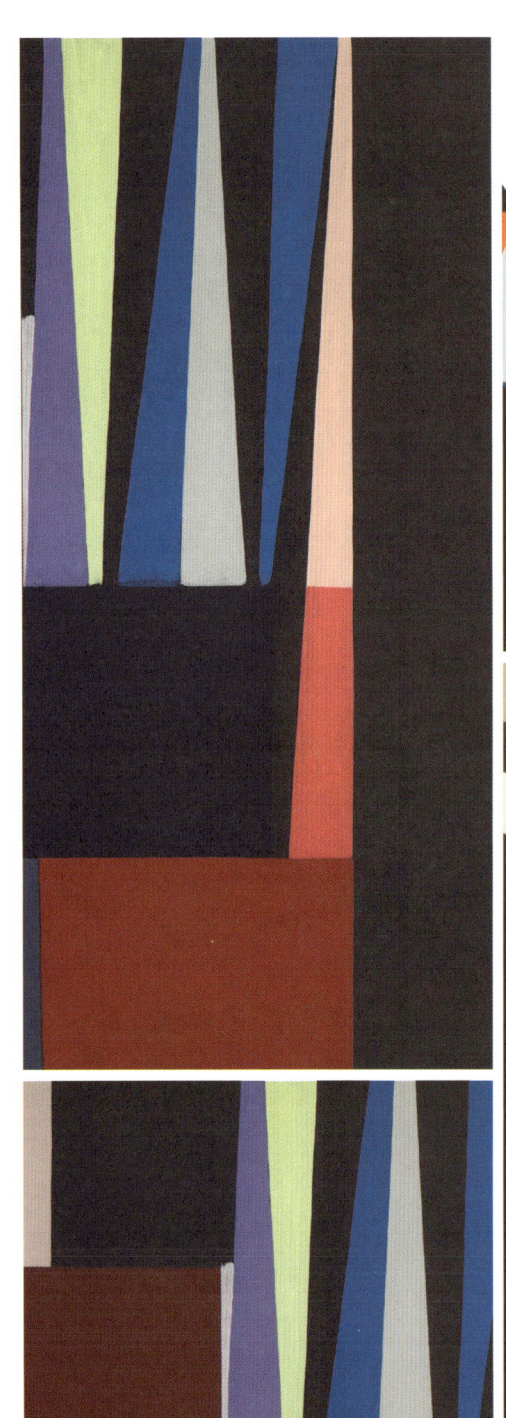

139

Red Blue Motion Totem 2010

Completion Date: 2010
Designer: Malene Landgreen
Photographer: Anders Sune Berg
Client: Esbjerg Kunstmuseeum, Denmark

141

Colour State

Completion Date: 2009
Designer: Malene Landgreen
Photographer: Anders Sune Berg
Client: Kunsthal Charlottenborg, Copenhagen, Denmark

- Wall Art
- Exhibit

143

• Wall Art • Exhibit •

144

145

Club Trouw Amsterdam III

- Wall Art
- Exhibit

Completion Date: 2010
Design Firm: Staynice
Photographer: Staynice
Client: Club Trouw, Amsterdam, the Netherlands

The hand-painted wall graphic work is a collaboration between 4 artists – Graphic Surgery, Erosie, Late and Staynice. The first layer was painted by Graphic Surgery, and the second layer was painted by Erosie and Late. The finishing of the project was done by Staynice and Graphic Surgery. The concept of the wall is to see how different forms and styles behave to one another.

Roger Mercury

Completion Date: 2010
Design Firm: Staynice
Photographer: Staynice
Client: Graphic Design Museum, Breda, the Netherlands

The hand-painted wall at the graphic design museum, Breda, the Netherlands is about the life of the hero Roger Mercury. The designer combines letters, geometric figure and human head felicitously.

The selection of orange, black and blue which set the basic tone of this painting with many tiny stars decorated on the background brings the visitors to a travel to firmament. Especially when the light was turned on in the night, it brings the visitors to a dreamlike and fantastic world.

The tridimensional diamond group makes it more stereoscopic, while the rectangles ranged in the same direction make the whole picture more harmonious and unified. What's more, the letters and the human head ornamented on the painting add a sense of beauty and fun. In a word, all these factors together present a spectacular and technological feeling.

- Wall Art
- Exhibit

149

Graphic Interpretation of Vlissingen

Completion Date: 2009
Design Firm: Staynice
Photographer: Staynice
Client: Kijkdoos, Vlissingen, the Netherlands

This hand-painted work is a graphic interpretation of the town Vlissingen, where the designer created this magic wall-painting. Just adopting five colours to exhibit an outline of the town, this work presents an imaginary world that offers mysterious and abstract space to fancy just by the expression of various and miscellaneous lines. These striking colour lumps seem to be hard to understand and recognize at the first sight, however, all the motifs are the refined annotation of daily life if observed in details.

Glasgow People

Completion Date: October 2009
Designer: Good Wives and Warriors
Photographer: Good Wives and Warriors
Client: Galleri Esplanaden, Copenhagen

This is a joint exhibition with other artists from Glasgow. The wall-painting was created directly onto the wall of the gallery in 2 days before the opening. Like all of their wall-paintings, the work only existed during the show and then it was painted over.

153

An Emphatic YES!

Completion Date: October 2010
Designer: Good Wives and Warriors, Giannina Capitani
Photographer: Good Wives and Warriors
Client: Personal collaborative exhibition with Giannina Capitani.

This cross-disciplinary installation marked the launch of Giannina Capitani's inaugural collection of knitted furniture and interior products. The textiles were combined with temporal wall and floor paintings by Good Wives and Warriors to create a multi-media, site-specific installation.

The installation combined the colourful geometric patterns of Capitani's knitted structures with the intense detail, natural forms and complex shapes of the paintings. Inspired by geometric and visual trickery, mathematical patterns and natural structures, this exhibition explored the juxtaposition of graphic imagery and the fluid anarchy of organic forms.

155

Talking about My Spontaneous Generation

Completion Date: August 2009
Designers: Good Wives and Warriors
Photographer: Mathew Stanton
Client: West Space Gallery, Melbourne, Australia

"Talking about My Spontaneous Generation" was painted directly onto the 4 walls and ceiling of a gallery space in Melbourne. It took 5 days to complete the wall-painting.

Like most of their works, the painting was developed from an obsession or idea based on a historical, scientific or technological reference point. The painting was ranged from organic and geometric line drawings to scientific imagery and complex natural structures.

Mixing the sophisticated stroke, perfect details and the black colour, the wall-painting brings people to a fantastic and magic world.

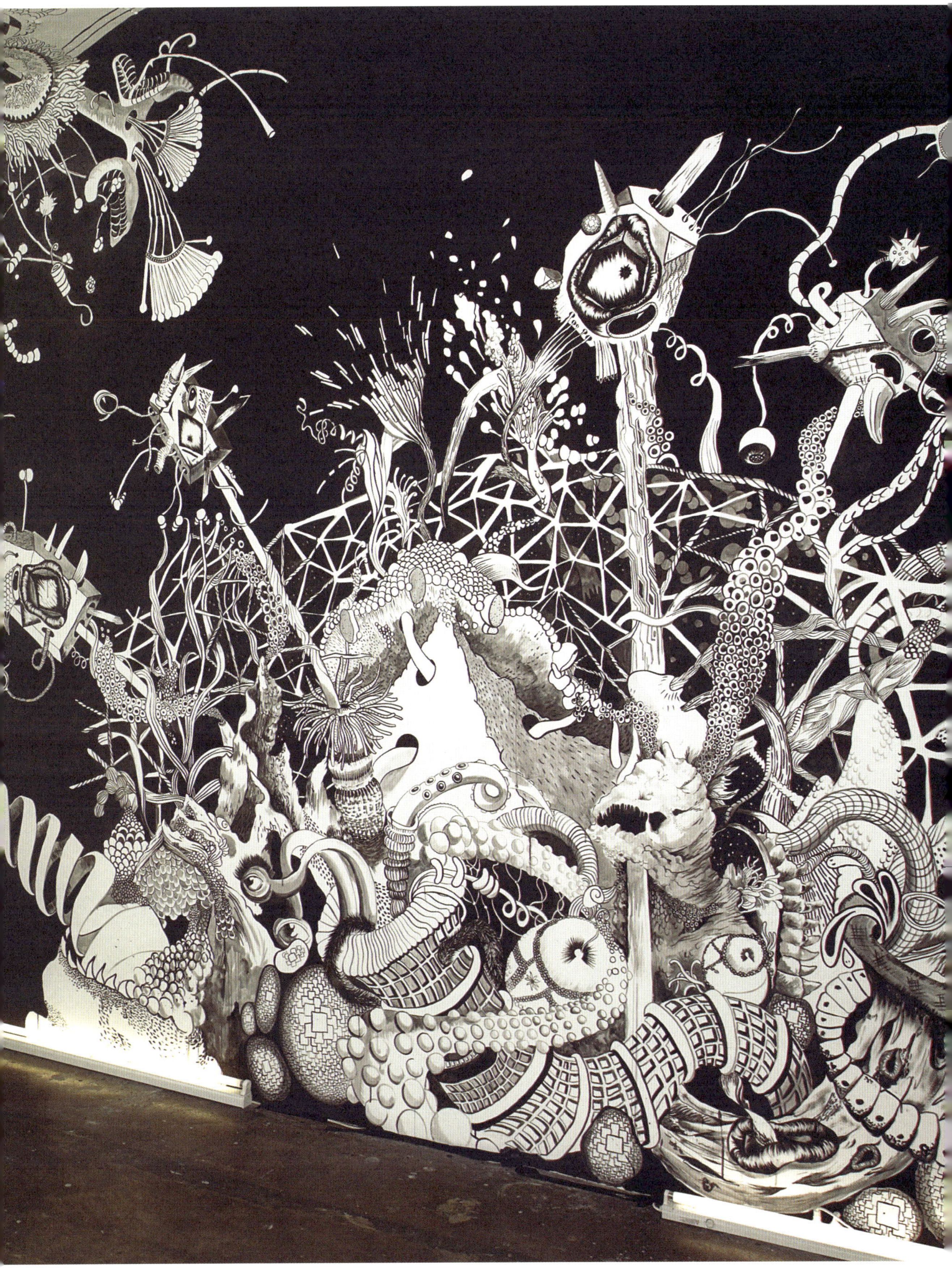

- Wall Art
- Exhibit

159

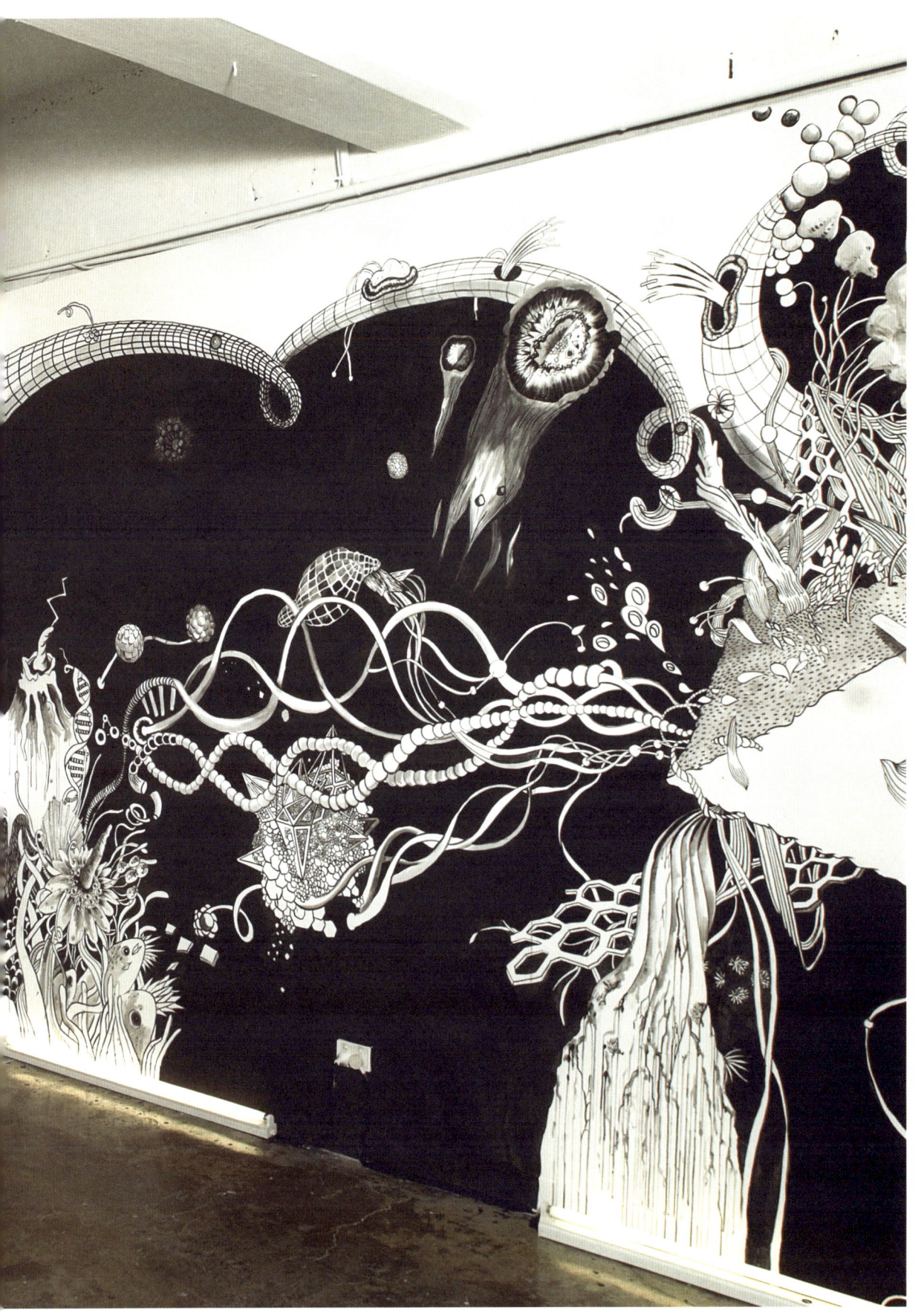

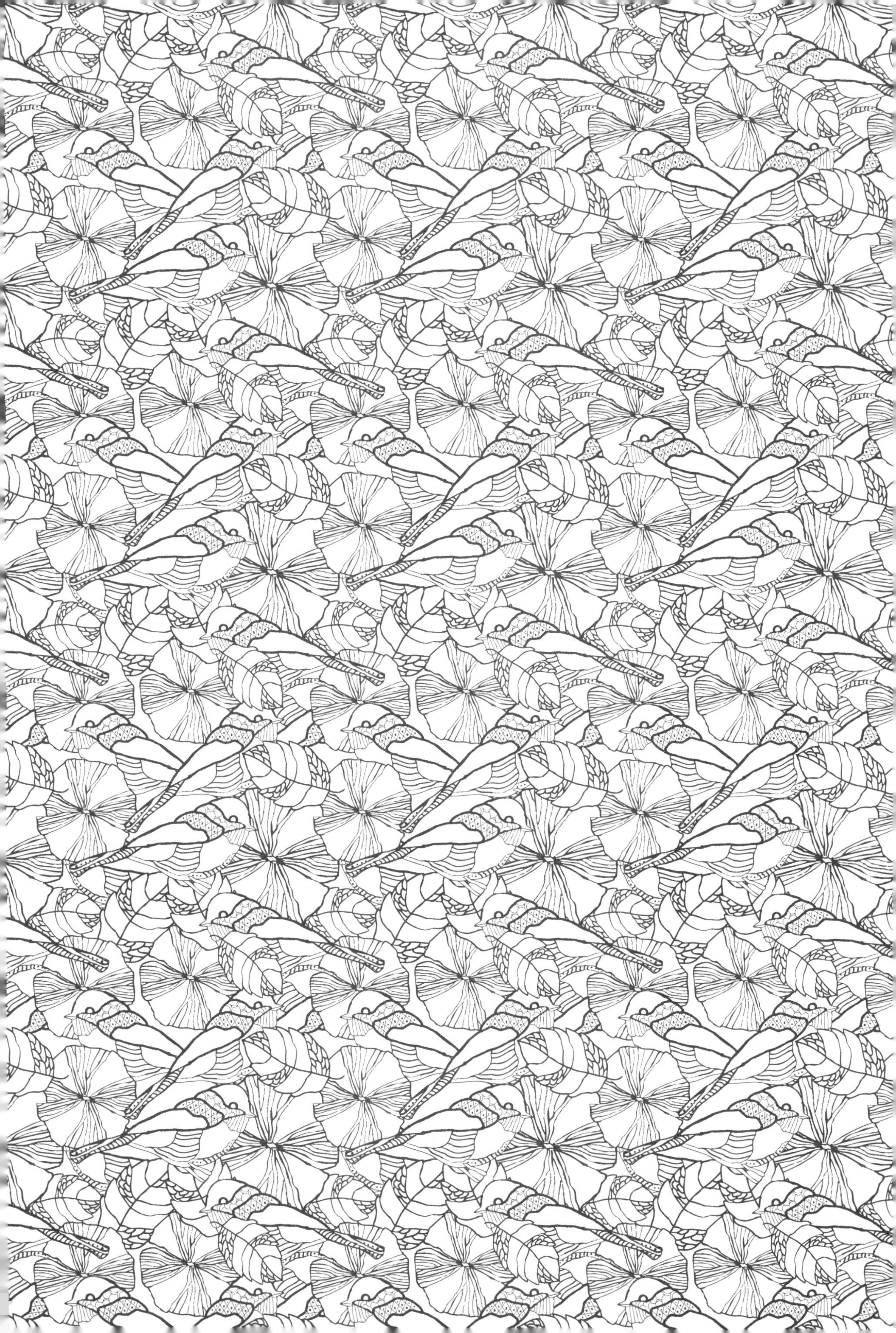

Wall Art • Home

Peonies, Lilies & Other Pretties

Completion Date: 2009
Designer: Abigail Borg
Photographer: Laura Edwards

Abigail Borg's debut wallpaper collection brings together selected designs from her award winning "Peonies, Lilies and Other Pretties" range. Abigail wanted to reiterate the unmistakeable characteristics of the Arts and Crafts Movement, emphasising shading and reducing elements down to their most concentrated form.

Each design in the collection is composed of a colour palette reflecting the shades used by designers at the turn of the 19th Century. With the collection being digitally printed, colours and details are not compromised, producing a modern approach to a vintage inspired wallpaper – perfect for individual panels or "feature" walls. Recently Abigail won an Elle Decoration award for Best British Pattern 2010.

163

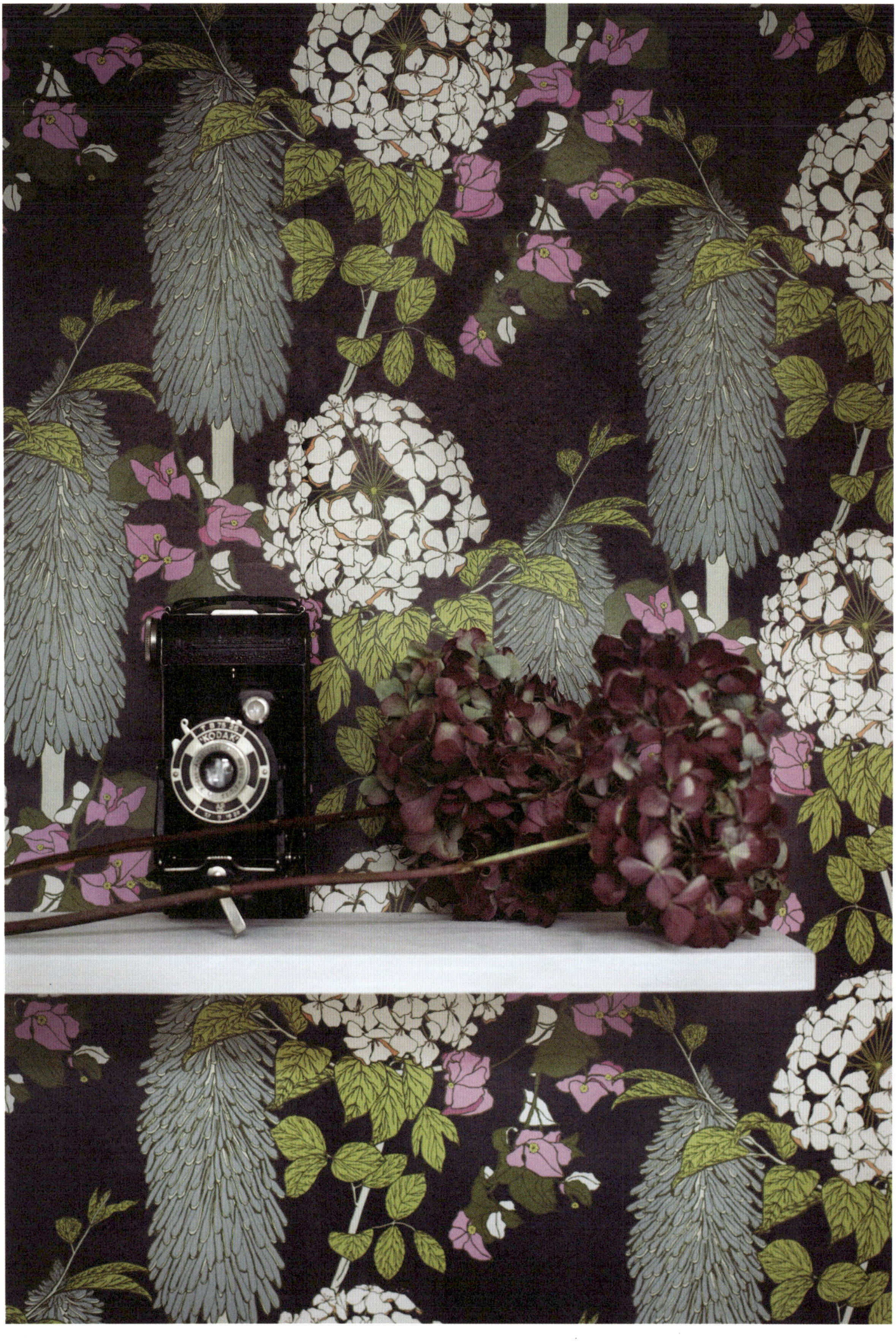
KODAK

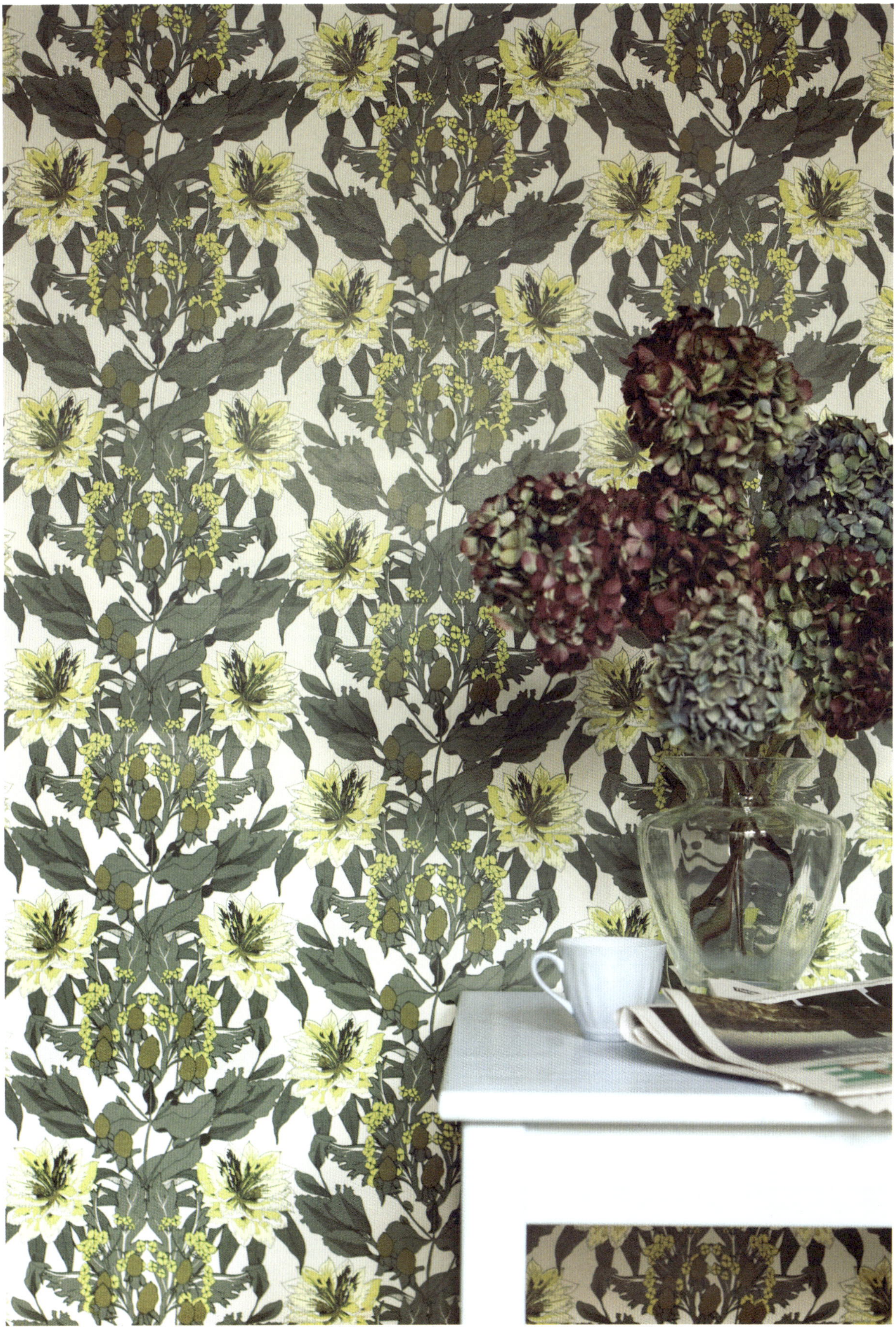

Walt Disney Signature

Completion Date: 2009
Design Firm: York Wall-coverings

Inspired by Walt Disney's timeless masterpiece Fantasia (1940), these wallpaper designs celebrate the visual beauty of nature, with beautiful plants, trees and leaves coming to magical life.

Keeping an exacting eye on trends while celebrating artistic works, the designers from York Wall-coverings lead a natural style which is unique, passionate and full of vitality. The pattern designs mixing beautiful shapes, soft colours and some elegant lines are not only outstanding backgrounds, but also exciting highlights in the space.

In addition, the collocation of elegant wallpaper and simple furnishings with comfortable and pleasant feeling offer space-saving solutions to interior design.

Masters Anniversary Edition

Completion Date: 2010
Design Firm: York Wall-coverings
Designer: Ronald Redding

In celebration of his remarkable 40-year-career in wall-covering design, Ronald Redding has selected some of his favorite designs and archival documents, masterfully blending past and present, to create an artistic collection of modern classics.

Stacy Garcia Luxury Wallpapers

Completion Date: 2008
Design Firm: York Wall-coverings
Designers: Stacy Garcia

The combination of innovative designs and bold colours are a trademark of renowned textile and accessory designer Stacy Garcia who produces inspiring and unexpected wallpapers for interiors.

The delicate and sumptuous patterns spreading on the wall match the dominated hue of the whole room well, and create a luxurious and gorgeous atmosphere.

169

Medley Design

Completion Date: 2009
Designer: Ronald Redding

Timeless designs inspired from Ronald Redding's treasured library of exclusive archival documents dating to the early 1800s.

Renowned for infusing classic designs with the exquisite colours and fresh interpretations, Ronald Redding creates gorgeous designs for today's most discerning interiors.

Contracted Wallpaper

Completion Date: 2006
Design Firm: Osborne&Little

This series of wallpaper adopts the repeated superposition of few simple elements, which creates a soft background for the rooms. The classic combination of yellow and champagne brings luxury and gorgeous style. The artful blend between furniture and wallpaper was achieved by using harmonious colours and textures.

Gorgeous Wallpaper

Completion Date: 2008-2009
Design Firm: Osborne&Little

The designers from Osborne&Little use fresh colours and beautiful patterns composed of exaggerated flowers and plants to match the same elegant light and furnishings, which presents a sense of luxuriance and magnificence. The pattern designs with the delicate and exquisite details also reflect the sufficiently high quality of the wallpaper.

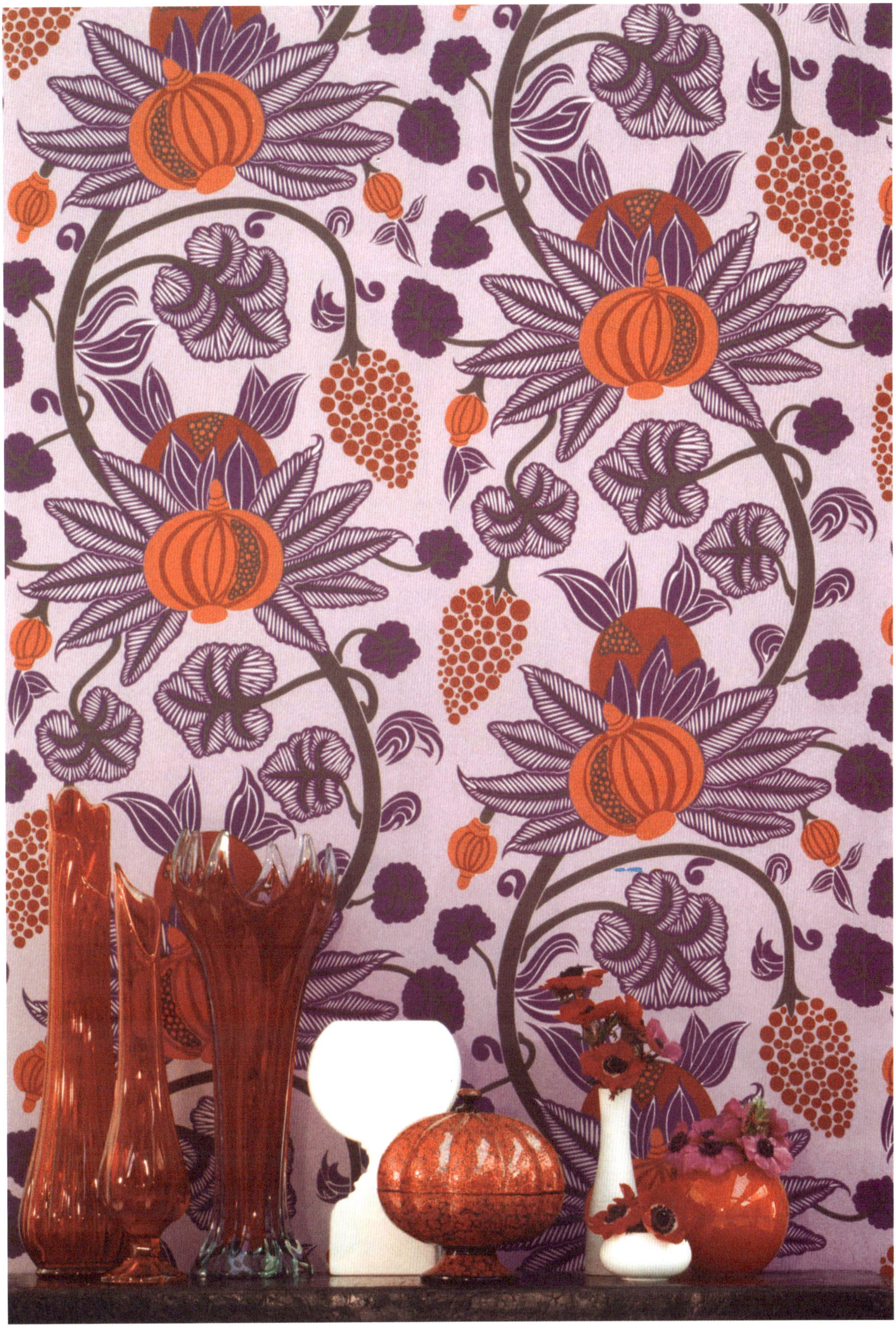

Walk in the Park Wallpaper

Completion Date: 2008
Design Firm: Osborne&Little

This unique and original design concept expresses a collection of fabrics and wallpaper which pays witty homage to the Englishman's love of both the native beauty and the exotica to be found in their rolling parklands. The designer uses white basic colour and black animal pattern to go with the white staircase and dim carpet perfectly.

Vintage Wallpaper

Completion Date: 2009
Design Firm: Osborne&Little

The designer of this wallpaper just adopts not more than three colours to go with the simple rectangular furnishing, which presents unadorned and tidy feeling to the whole room. The pattern design and the paper crane are elegant and refined.

Sumptuous Wallpaper

Completion Date: 2008-2009
Design Firm: Osborne&Little

The design concept of these wallpapers originates in baroque style decoration. Matching the luxury curtain and bedding pretty well, the above wallpaper with beautiful patterns and textures looks delicate, imposing and palatial. While as a background, the colour tone of the below one set off the retro furniture very harmonious, and the pattern design is plain without any miscellaneous decoration, which presents a sense of neatness and elegance.

Natural Wallpaper

Completion Date: 2008
Design Firm: Osborne&Little

The designer pursues a natural style by using the pattern composed of trees and leaves to create a artistic and elegant work. The leaves with hand-drawing style are the basic elements of left one which adopts warmer colours to match the furniture in same colour tone and makes the whole room in perfect harmony. While the right one with the vivid tree patterns in tidy order throughout collocates the modest furniture to bring a country garden style.

Pompadour Wallpapers

Completion Date: 2008
Design Firm: Osborne&Little

This set of wallpaper adopts bright green colour to match the bedding and furniture in the room, which makes the decorations design in perfect harmony. As for the pattern design, both of them are delicate and concentrated on details portraying. The whole works present a style that is timeless, unique, original and is not influenced by changing trends.

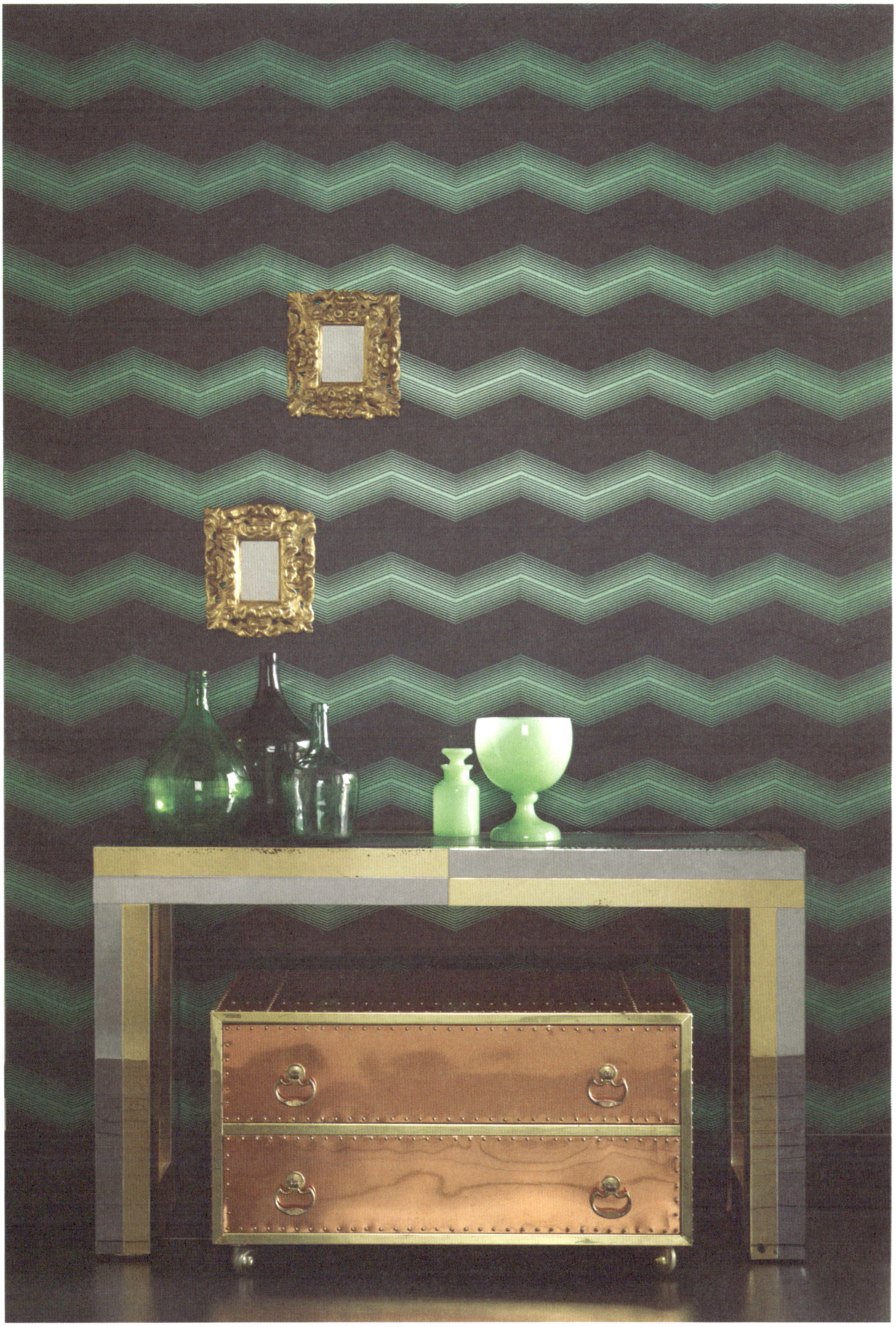

Aimee Wilder Wallpaper

Completion Date: 2010
Designers: Aimee Wilder
Photographer: Neasdarand
Client: Masdauda

The series of designs were created by Aimee Wilder to form a collection of works between 2001 and today. Aimee decided to create the "Aimee Wilder" brand and produced many of the designs as a signature handprinted wallpaper product, and will continue each year to expand her current range.

All these designs add a classic modern approach to the wall-coverings available today. The designs are meant to be creative, cutting-edge and timeless.

181

lazer
studios and lofts - one room living
Lucian Freud
Rolling Stone THE 500 GREATEST ALBUMS OF ALL TIME
Andrew Wyeth
FRANCESCA WOODMAN
FACE TO FACE
All the etchings of Rembrandt
DAMIEN HIRST
BRUCE WEBER
VOGUE
HERBERT LIST
EXITS
EDWARD LEAR'S BIRDS
RICHARD AVEDON EVIDENCE 1944-1994
A Second Decade of Guess Images 1991 to 2001

ORGASMIUM
DONTEATRA
NIMFAPAM
ILLUMATIN
DEXAZENICA
EUPHORITAL
ELIXITOX
RENOVOGENE
Focuset
SOMNITOL
RIDANOREX
STRESSADONE
LOBOTAMINE
Lurmatap
Cymbyalter
Lieagra
Dopephedrine
Vitalitol
WILDER
FASHION NOW
ATCHBOX LABELS
HOUSES
S OF TRACE
aude cahun marcel moore
ROBERT CRUMB

- Wall Art • Home •

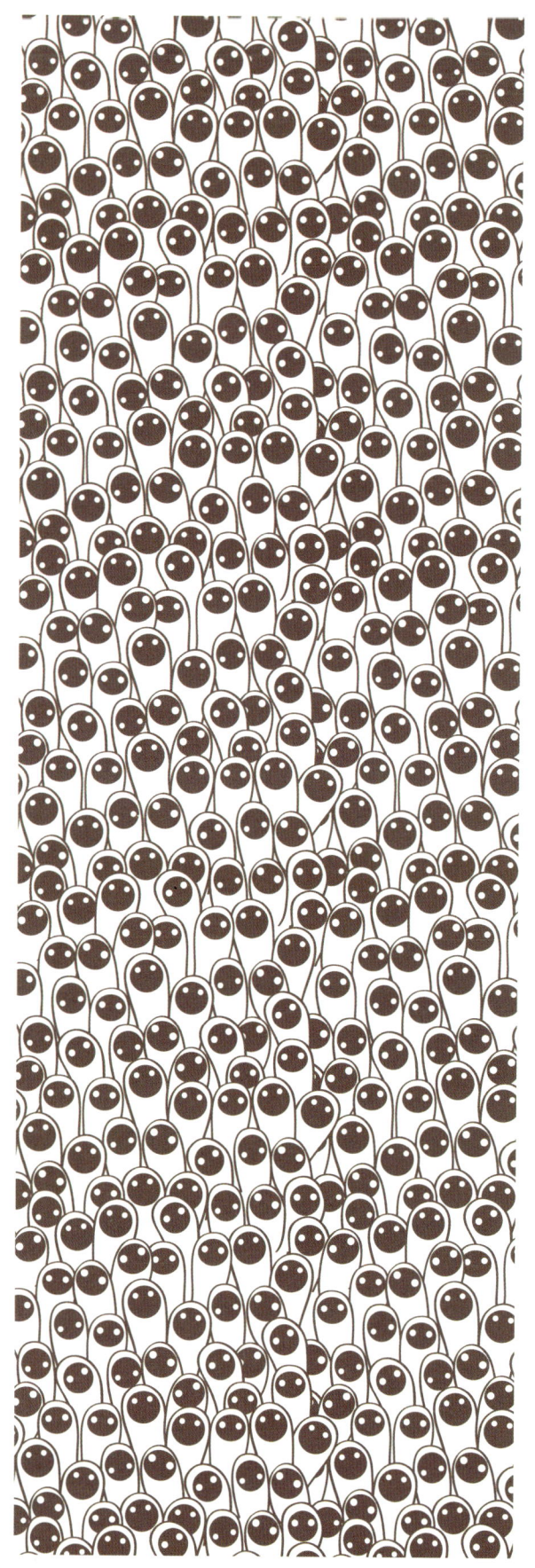

Circle Art

Completion Date: 2007
Designer: Urszula Bogucka
Photographer: Urszula Bogucka
Client: Jannelli & Volpi

Created for the Milan shop of Janelli & Volpi, the wallpaper design was decoratively printed for the decoration of some rooms and clubs.

The geometric pattern was constructed from duplication of circles which is the basic form of the design and created hypnotic wavy lines.

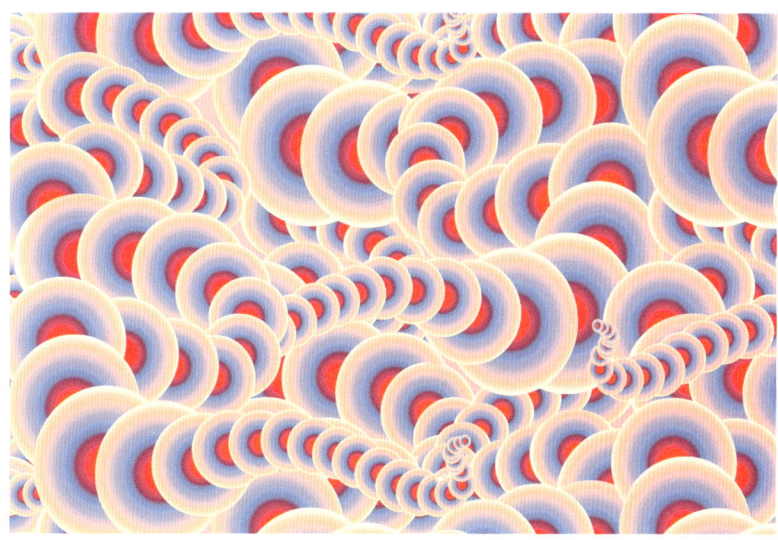

Svärmor Wallpapers

Design Firm: Studio Lisa Bengtsson
Designer: Lisa Bengtsson

Hosting the latest fashion scene, these wallpapers provide a stylish setting for fans of society tidal current by elements that are strictly suitable for modern ladies, such as the confident Prima Ballerina and exquisite shoes. These wallpapers whose details express the charm of retro style, create outstanding backgrounds for the space. It is advisable to place different sizes or directions to get beautiful designs full of variety and delight.

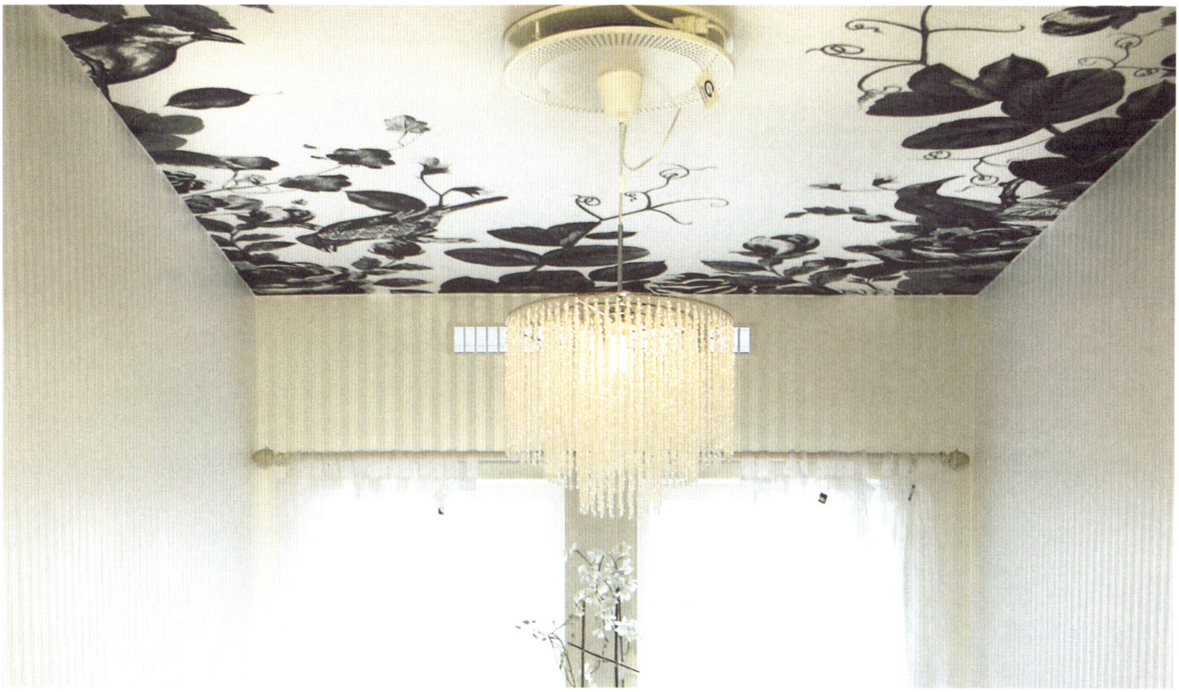

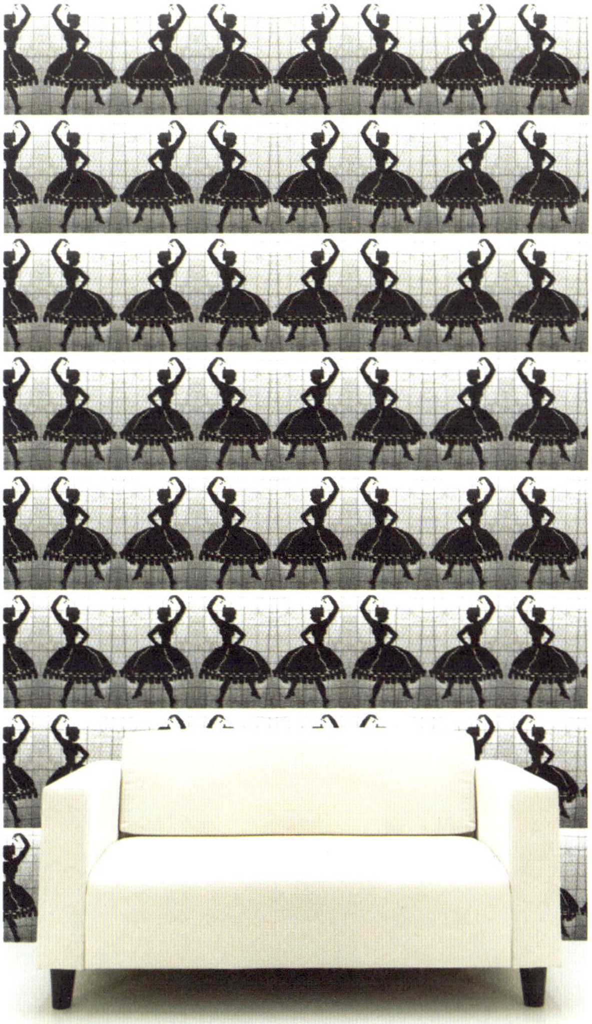

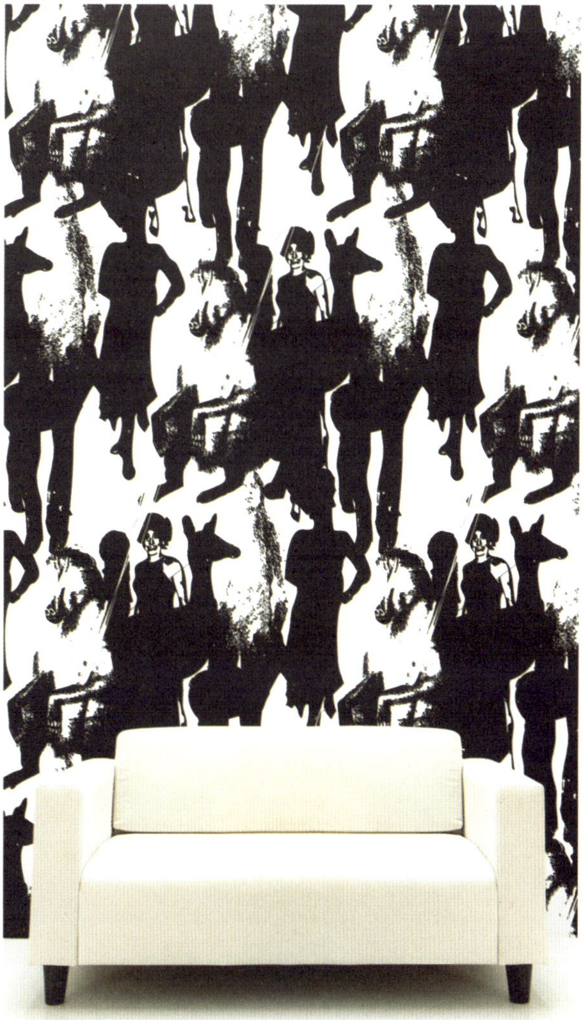

Lady of Easy Virtue

Completion Date: 2008-2009
Design Firm: Studio Lisa Bengtsson
Designer: Lisa Bengtsson

What greets you is an artistic and beautiful world with gorgeous oil painting portraits and flowers, taking you back to the Middle Ages of Europe, when designers enjoyed the use of bright-colour patterns or paintings to express glory, honor, and wealth. The design has dreamt up a refreshing concept with a lack of organization, presenting a new appearance of some simple patterns.

News

Completion Date: 2009
Design Firm: Studio Lisa Bengtsson
Designer: Lisa Bengtsson

Staying true to the design theme, the old newspapers pattern also features retro trends, with simple black and white colour, where exists a kind of low-key luxury instead of making people feel monotonous.

La Vie En Rose & Rosmarie

Completion Date: 2009
Design Firm: Studio Lisa Bengtsson
Designer: Lisa Bengtsson

In Lisa's well-defined fabrics collection, colours and details are made to enhance the beauty of the nature to see and record fragments of our life and world, suitable for furniture in different styles.

With less trace of modern design, each pattern is precise and perfect, featuring the red colour, alternated with details in dark yellow. Specially developed fabrics include Linen, Canvas, and cotton, which highlight the noble temperament and what you get is a home resembles the old movie scene.

Baronessa

Completion Date: 2010
Design Firm: Studio Lisa Bengtsson
Designer: Lisa Bengtsson

It is a new work created in 2010. Combined with elegant colours and gorgeous flower patterns, the fabrics for wall decoration remind you the classic European style in Middle Ages.

N-pool

Completion Date: 2009
Designer: Nawer
Photographer: Olga Borda
Client: Private

Wall mounted graphics at the entrance of a private apartment. Colour contrasts, composition of shapes and surfaces, presented through perspective and axonometry, create depth and optically expand the space.

Colour, as the main medium of the graphics, continues the flow by engulfing installation elements, which becomes inseparable fragments of the presentation. The creative graphics are designed by the use of spray paint, masking tape and stencils.

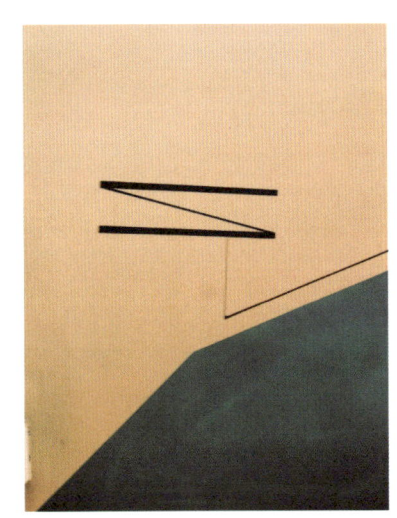

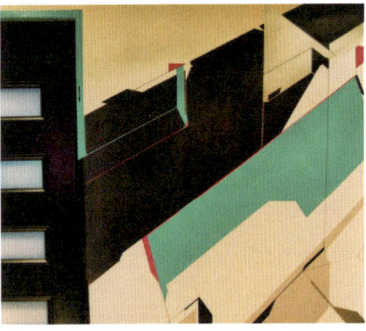

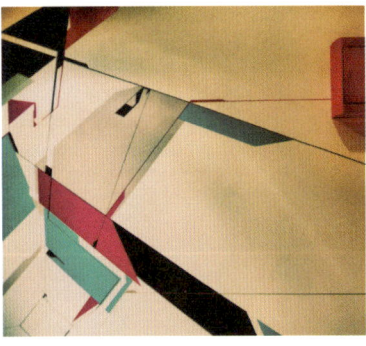

193

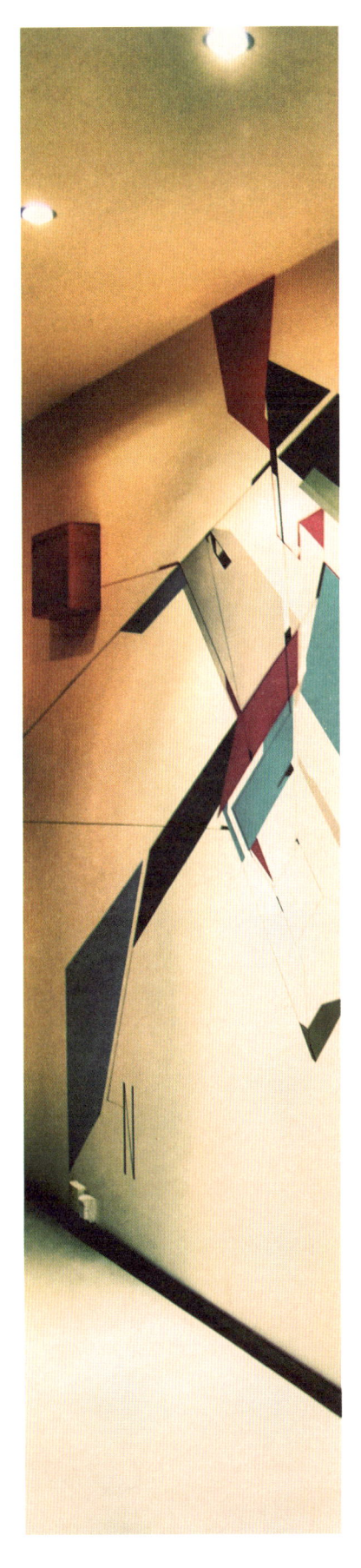

Point36.6

Completion Date: 2010
Designers: Nawer & Ariel
Photographer: Nawer
Client: Private

Interior wall mounted graphics within a private apartment located in the Krakow city center, where the conscious application of a monotone chromatic colour palette together with acute colour accents creates a strong contrast with the raw white walls of the space.

Using axonometry and perspective, the structural composition of lines, surfaces and points add a dynamic to the static modern interior space.

The fluorescent lighting adds a unique spatiality by emitting a neutral colour appearance, which becomes a pulsing interactive element shaping the space.

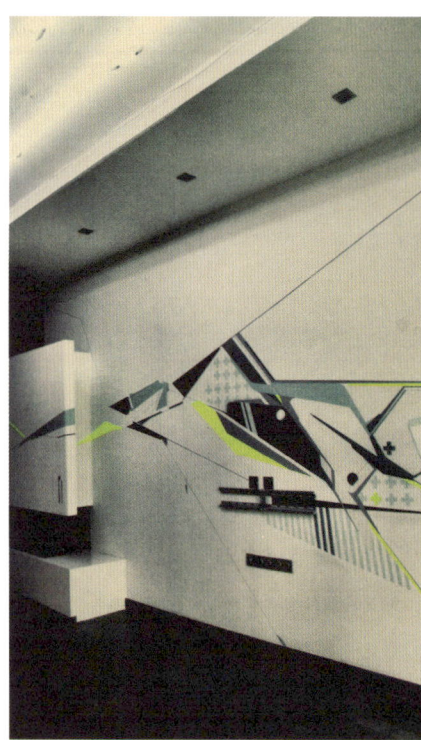

195

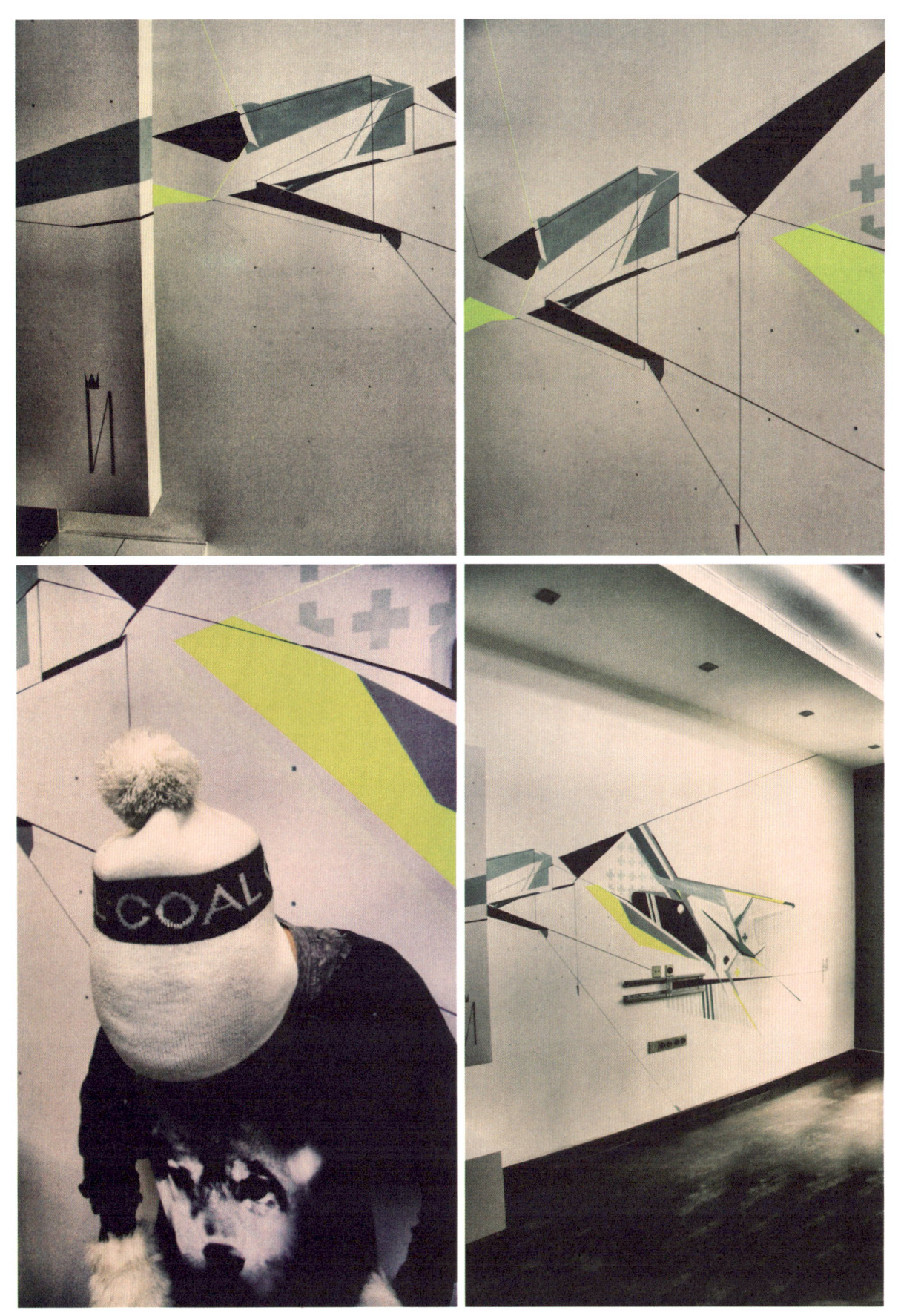

Midia Effects Design Studio

Completion Date: 2008
Designer: Carol Rivello
Photographers: Carol Rivello, Thomas Ventura
Client: Midia Effects

Midia effects is a south Brazilian digital studio that initiated its activities in 2000. Their expertise is web, video, special effects, new medias and everything you can imagine. Carol was currently working with midiaeffects when they decided to move into a bigger place, and he was asked to develop a series of illustrations to make the new studio a really fun place to work at. The result is the midiaeffects interior design project.

The history behind the zipper illustration is really cute. Their previous studio was small, but had an amazing view of the whole city. The new place is amazing, but there are neither many windows nor lovely view anymore. In order to make an homage to the previous place, Carol created a zipper that opened the wall and showed a stylized version of the city. For the chill out lounge, a pink world with sheep and comic sleeping balloons was created. The TV was turned into a mad robot and the shelves dripped pink paint. The fire pole was turned into a fun candy can, with stripes and dancing chocolates.

197

This is a small project with a short timescale. The designers were requested to brighten up a dark and small powder room. As a huge street art aficionado, the client requested the specific imagery, which is based upon an illustration they had produced 2 years ago. The designer really wanted to give the project a more street-styled vibe with crazy colours and distinctive lines.

The way they personalised the work, is to use a contrasting palette of fluorescent pastel colours against the dark blue base coat. The remaining area, on that particular floor is predominantly white washed.

The main idea was to create energy and colour, which allows the room to be instantly viewed with surprise and shock. This used a mixture of elements, character design and distinctive features. Even the toilet seat was transformed into a large pocket watch. Clouds floated across the window and the Cheshire cat grinned at you on the back wall and was also reflected on the mirror exposing his Swarovski embedded tooth.

Alice in Dreamland Wall-painting

Completion Date: 2010
Design Firm: Miss Led
Designers: Jim Sutherland, Gareth Howat
Photographer: Gareth
Client: Meg Mathews

199

E-glue

Completion Date: 2008-2010
Design Firm: E-glue
Designers: Marielle Baldelli, Sébastien Messerschmidt

Considering space as a blank page, e-glue brings illustration for kids to life with a range of contemporary graphic designs featuring favourites such as savanna, jungle, pirates, underwater world, train, robots, princesses, dinosaurs and many more ! Offering a wide catalogue regularly enriched with new decorative stickers, E-glue proposes theme packs or single giant decals to adapt to the children's spaces.

E-glue wall decals are made in France from solid colour material that is laser cut (not printed) into shapes. The colours are much richer and the material is also very thin, so it lays beautifully on surfaces for a realistic look as if it were painted on the wall.

201

Wall Art • Home

203

Wall Art • Home

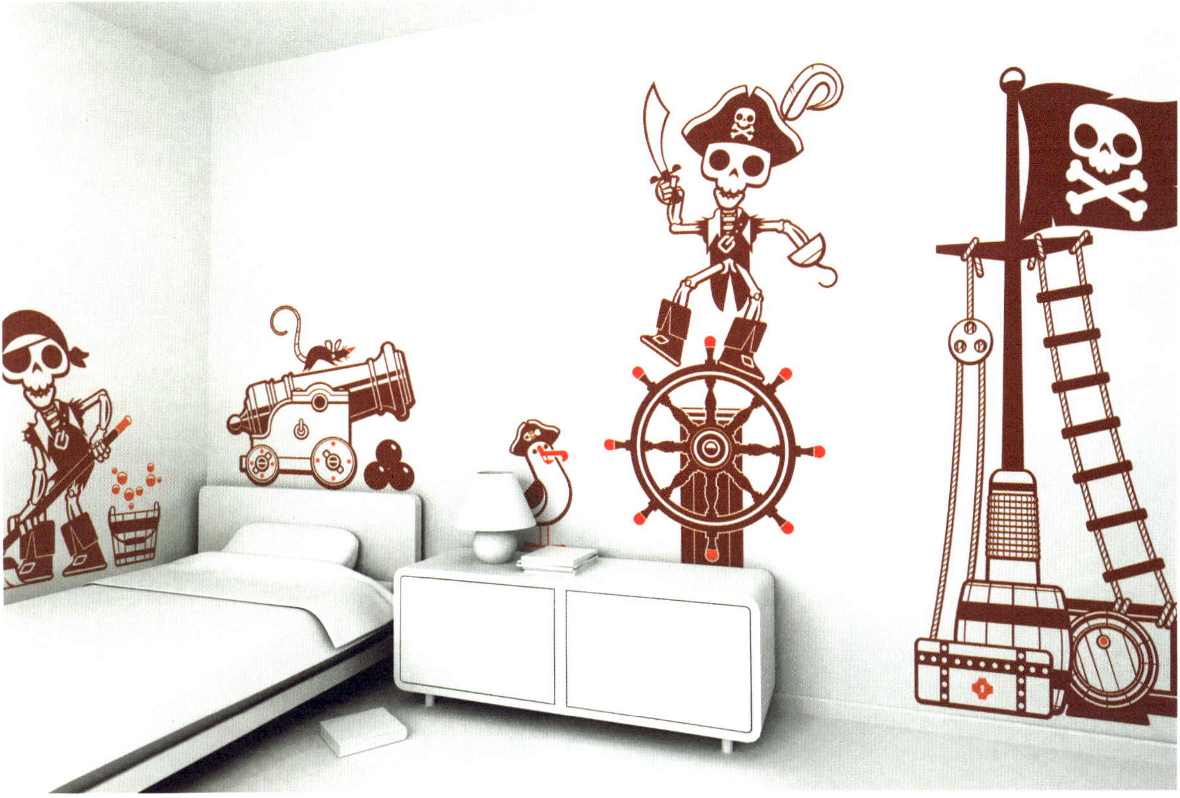

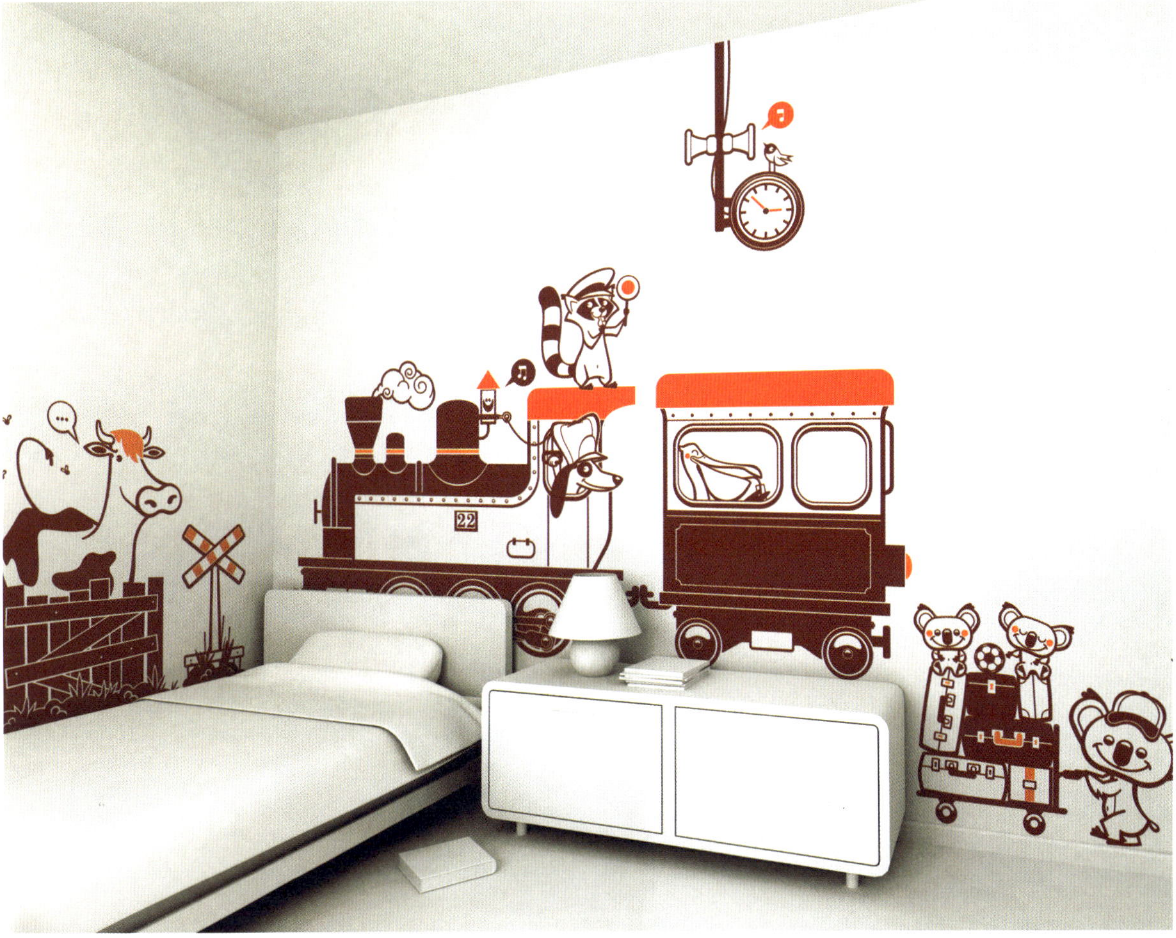
22

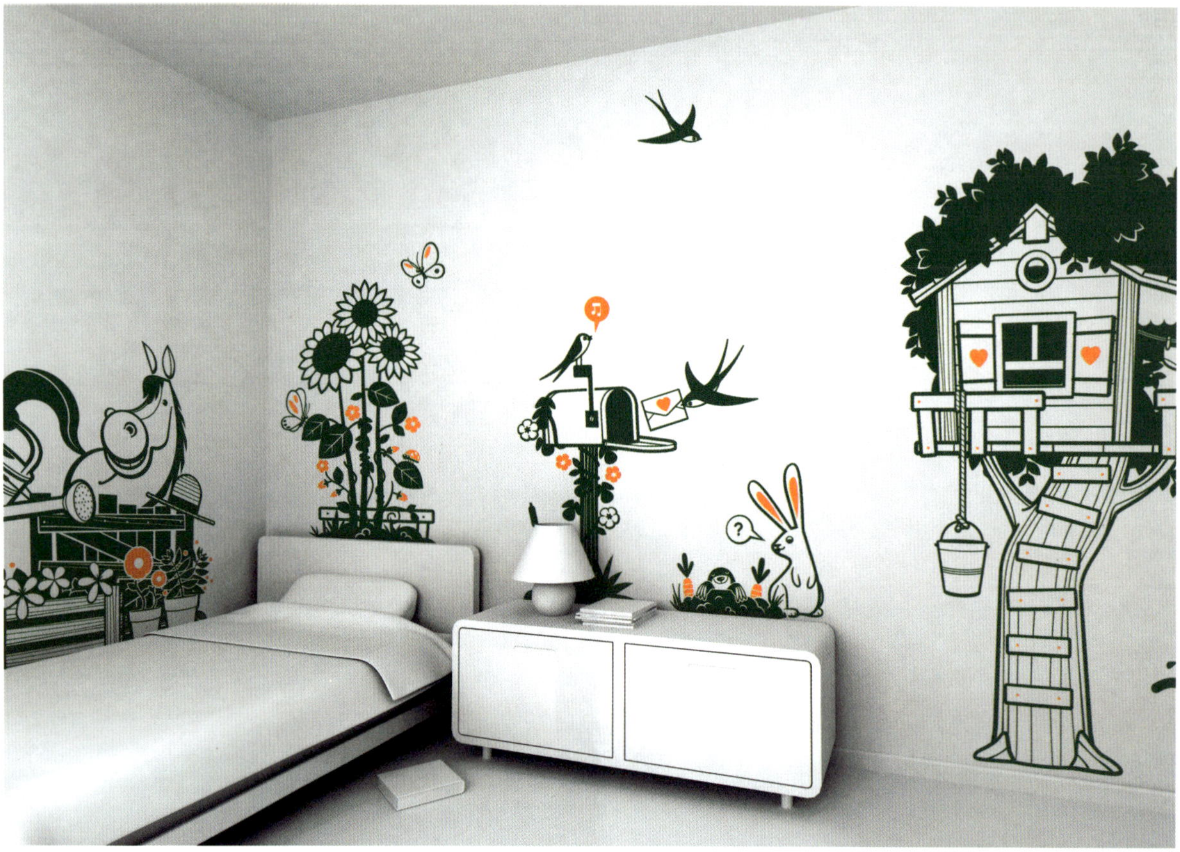

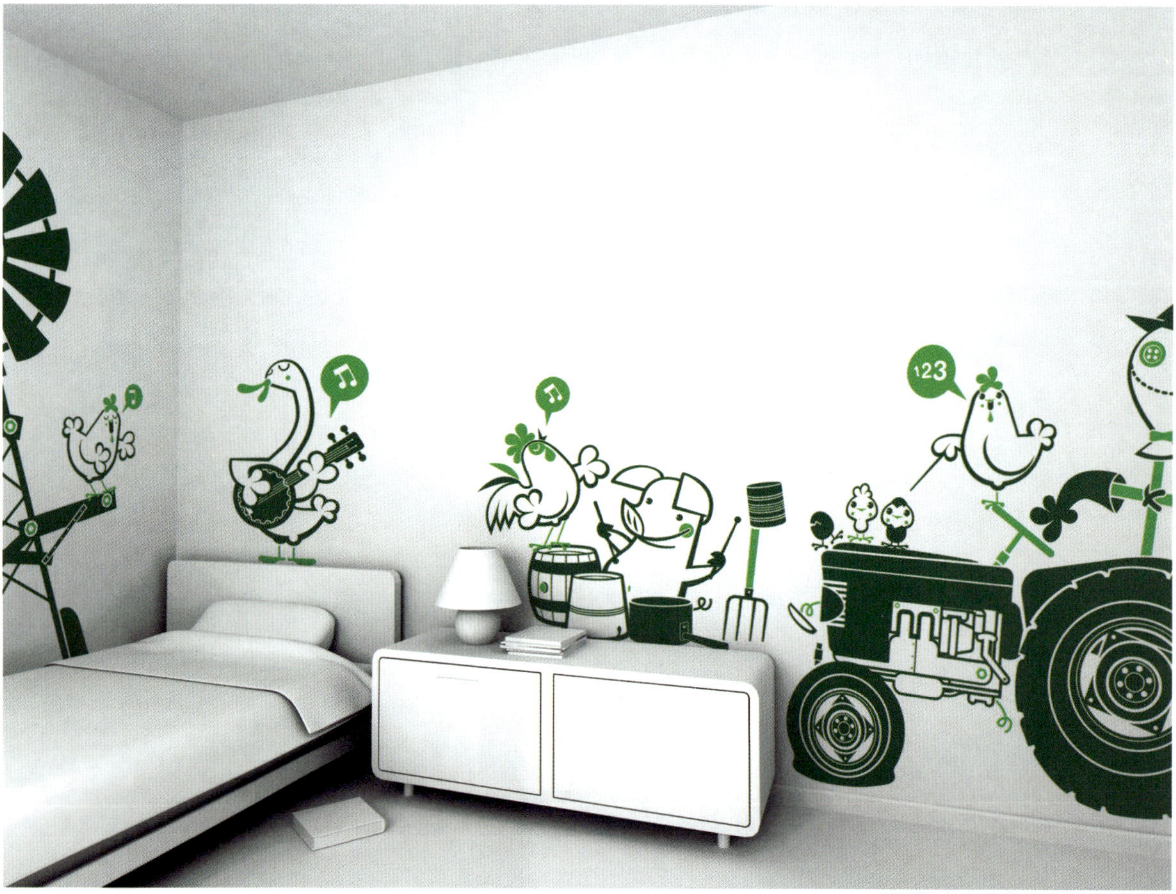
123

207

Viernes De Animas Movie Set

Movie set design for a Mexican production of a horror mystery film called "Viernes De Animas" which translates loosely into holy Friday. This was supposed to be the interior of an abandoned victorian mansion. The different textures were done by using acrylic paints, stencils and different kinds of papers. Every surface of the house where it was filmed was painted and transformed.

Completion Date: 2008
Designer: Victor Sandoval
Photographer: Victor Sandova
Client: Baja Productions

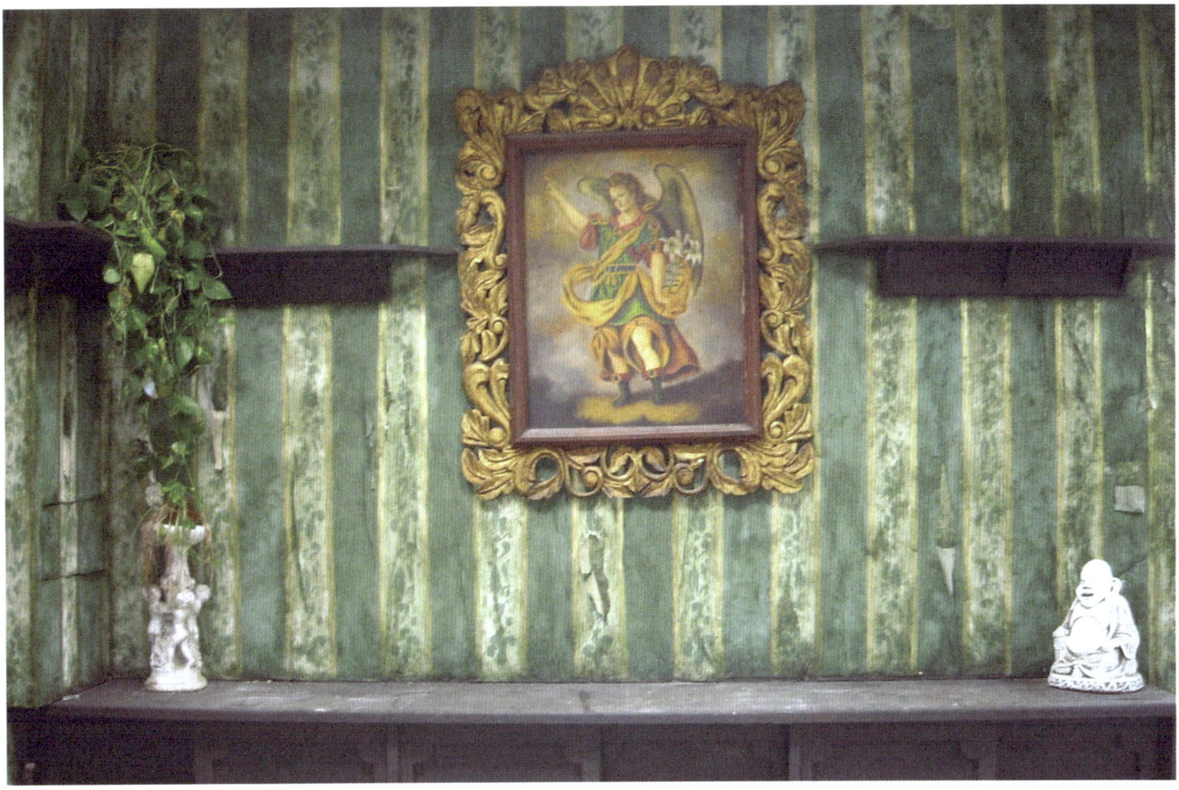

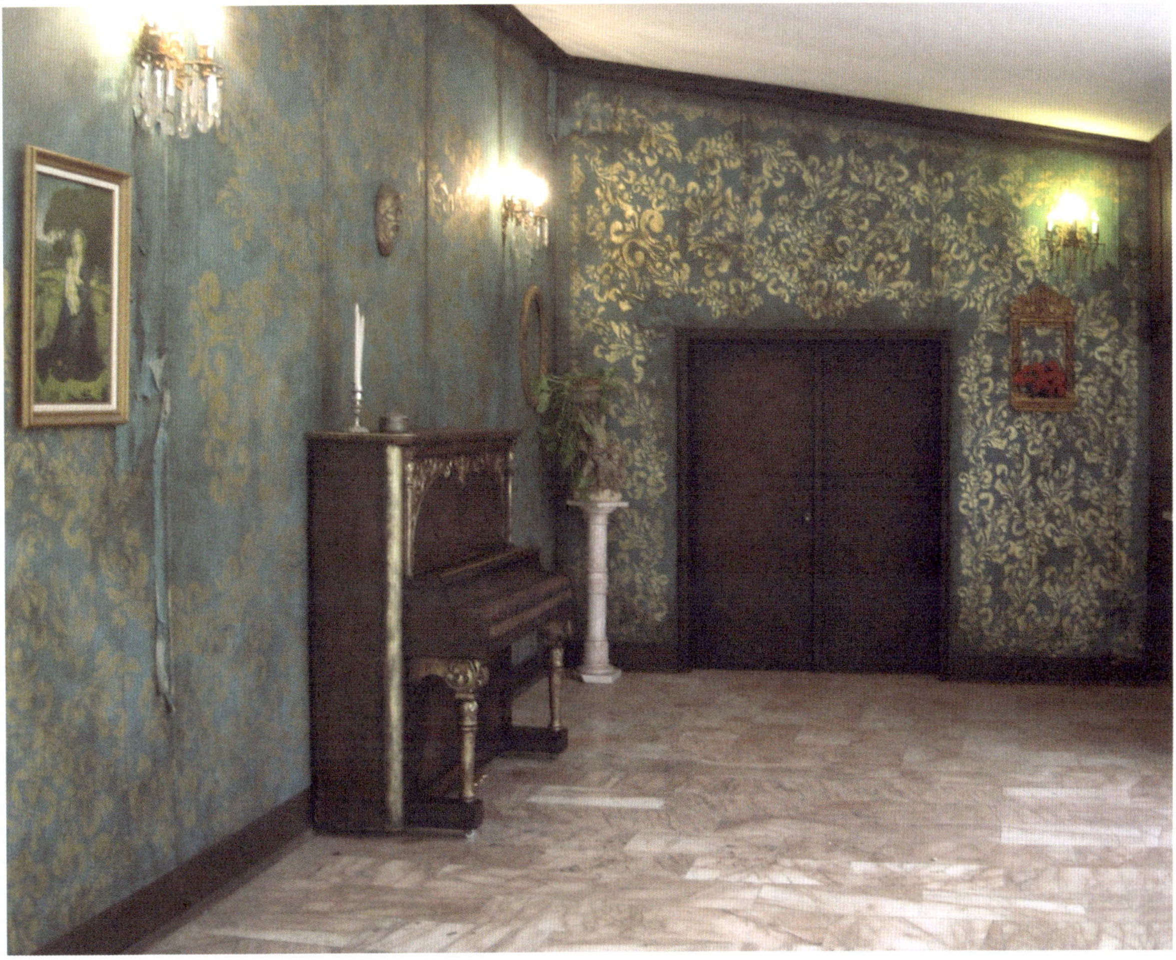

Mural Gris

Completion Date: 2008
Design Firm: Reaktor Lab
Designer: Jorge Aguilar
Photographer: Ema Urbina

This work was inspired by the living way of human beings. Most people believe that the world can be destroyed as the consequences of bad living habits (pollution for example). This is the designer's egocentric point of view. This mural exposes the vulnerability of man to nature.

This piece of wall-painting only selects two colours, white and gray, to express a meaningful point even though the line is simple without many redundant varieties and the colour is also a little monotonous.

The whole picture presents us a profound space to meditate. Under the paintbrush of the designer, our nature mother is just like a tender and amiable female. However, if we human being had done something that hurt her, she may change her countenance immediately and return us a painful lesson by the restless billowing waves that seems to submerge us at any moment.

Mural Azul

Completion Date: 2008
Design Firm: Reaktor Lab
Designer: Jorge Aguilar
Photographer: Nelida Ahedo
Client: Albert Chermayeff

This mural is a full project that Jorge Aguilar was assigned to it's entirety, from concept and proposal of colours to the design of the furniture.

The choice of graphics and colours was carefully made to maintain a harmonious environment that causes reflexive moments. This space is meant to be enjoyable for a long time without overwhelming the senses.

Golden Drops

Completion Date: 2009
Designer: Olefir Zoya

Fireplace decorative wall (panno) is made of gypsum drops of unusual forms, glass beads and some metal details. Experimenting with materials and shapes enriches the texture of this piece of decoration.

Contemporary simplicity and emotionally-spiritual depth is the message of this project. The rich colour schemes create a sense of calmness and peacefulness for the space.

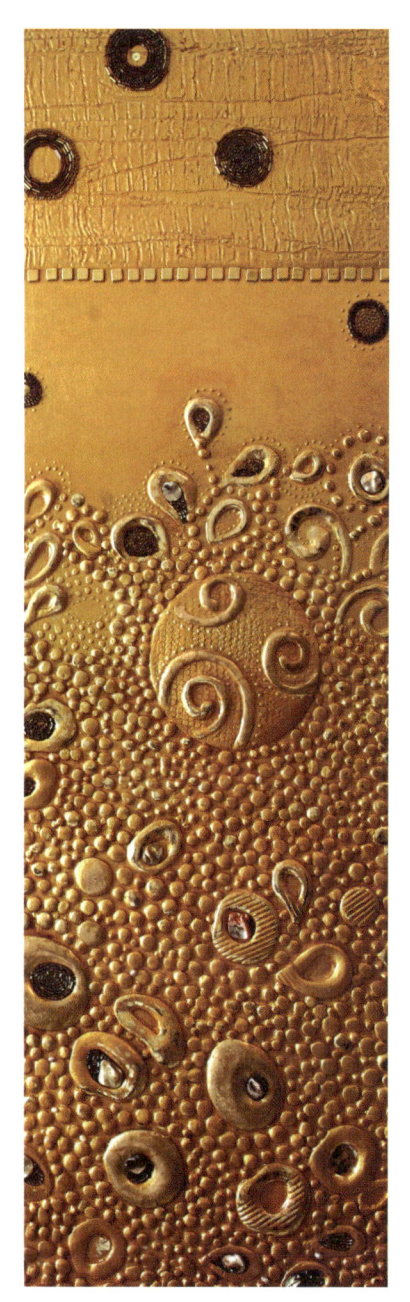

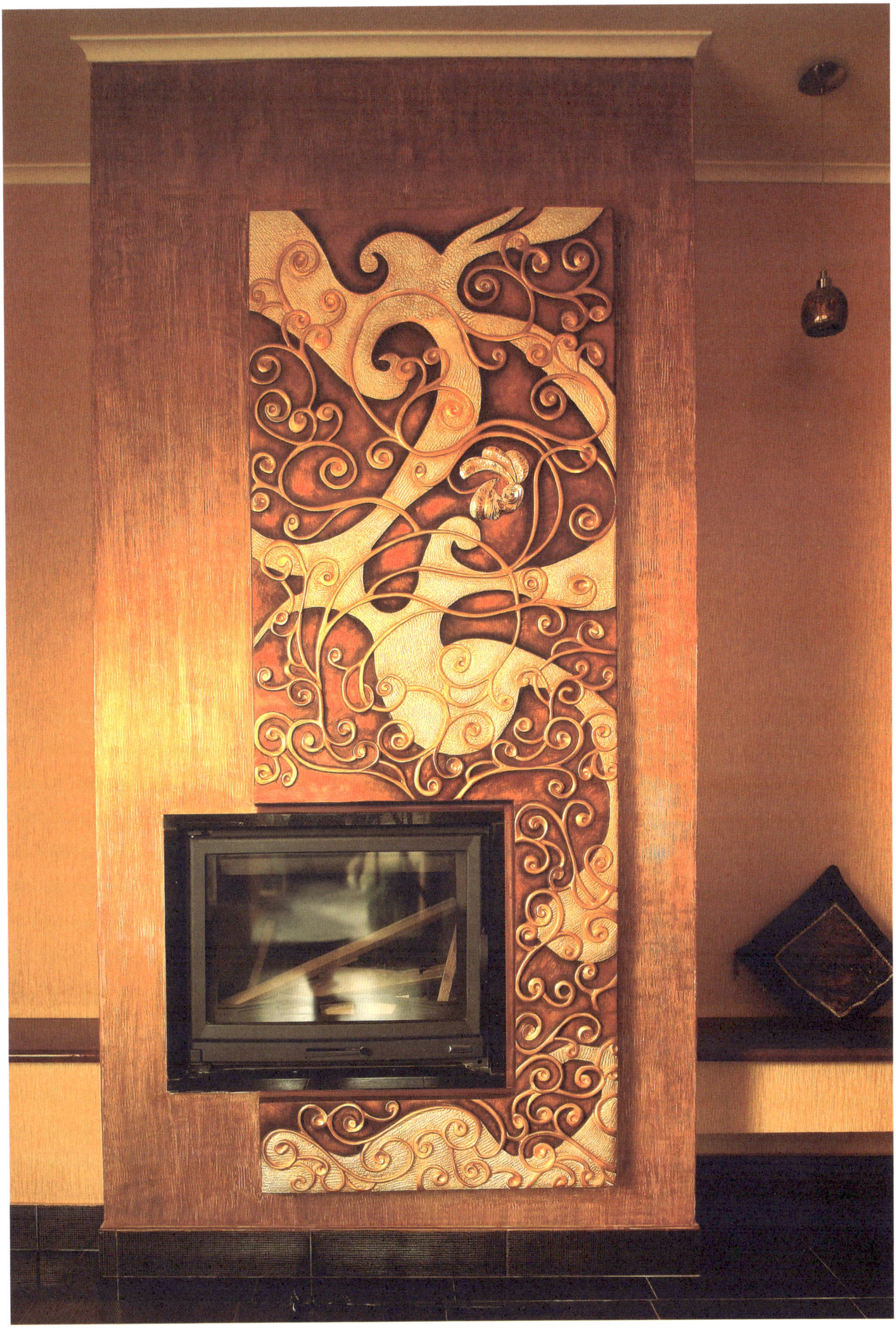

Naive

Completion Date: 2010
Designer: Olefir Zoya
Photographer: Taras Ivankiv

In morden world where technologies are very developed, the simple and basic things that have a human touch have been encouraged more and more. The main task of this work is to bring a note of emotion in the minimalist interior. Decision is to create a bright decorative panno with deep relief fills glass Beads. Naive, simple idea of panno is basic feature of this project.

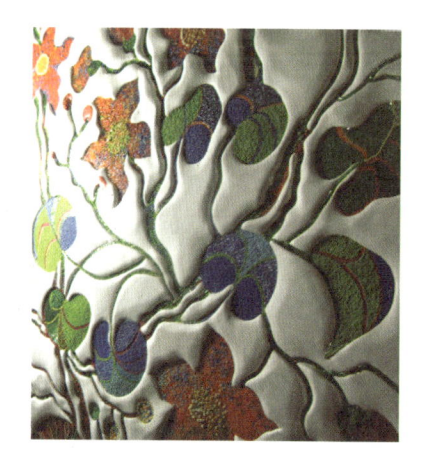

215

Wall-painting of Bizarre Animals

Completion Date: 2010
Design Firm: RR Army Studio
Designers: Ibie, Edjinn
Photographer: RR Army Studio

The designer adopts bold imagination to present a fantastic world to us. Both of these two pieces of wall-paintings' main body is a bizarre and magic dragon.

The upper one adopts white and black colour as the basic hue and makes the backgrounds go with the bedding preferably, which presents a feeling of mysterious world around. The two yellow elliptic fire balls adjust the dim hue of the whole image and add something bright to it.

As for the below one, some bright colours are used to paint the piled semicircular figures mixing some cartoon characters like SpongeBob, vivid cave with bubble and green dragon. All these elements make the whole wall-paintings interesting and creative.

Wall-painting & Collage Art

Completion Date: 2010
Design Firm: RR Army Studio
Designers: Ibie, Edjinn
Photographer: RR Army Studio

The concept of the paintings along the wall of staircase is inspired by collage art. The bright colours and lovely figures were adopted to decorate the space. The characters featured here are rather interesting and abstract, and the combination of these fresh colours gives a sense of passion and outstanding feeling.

In the rooms, many creative features are mixed together freely and arbitrarily, such as the funny woman head, strange animal bodies head and lovely letters. Especially the plump characters and the cartoon figures are portrayed as cute, which adds a sense of fun and interest to the interior rooms.

This set of works turns out to be vivid and grotesque. They also bring unlimited vibrant atmosphere to the limited space.

Wall Art • Home

219

Lovely Wall Sticker Designs

Completion Date: 2009
Designers: Vêro Escalante
Photographer: Gareth
Client: Wallkiss Decorative Vinyls

Merging various lovely design elements, such as the little black cat, butterfly and string ball besides the goldfish bowl, these ingenious wall stickers are blended in the interior decoration harmoniously and make the whole room cute.

Other motifs such as the little watering pot above the flower, the lovely clock and the vivacious bird cage all go with the nearby furniture perfectly. While pretty horse and vines stickers present a playful sense to the simple furniture successfully.

221

Sticker: Metre

Completion Date: 2010
Design Firm: Woozy
Photographer: Woozy

It is a functional and creative sticker, designed for children who can play with their high.

Sticker: Life

Completion Date: 2010
Design Firm: Woozy
Photographer: Woozy

This sticker design titled "Life" shows the idea of the life through a microscope.

Sticker: Branches

Completion Date: 2009
Design Firm: Woozy
Photographer: Woozy

The inspiration for branches came from the skeleton of the tree branches, designed in an abstract way.

Sticker: Floreal & Okapi

Completion Date: 2009-2010
Design Firm: Woozy
Photographer: Woozy

The works have been designed with an organic shape in relation with the nature, and structured in a dynamic movement. Both this two wall stickers reflect the natural concept to present a comportable and fresh feeling.

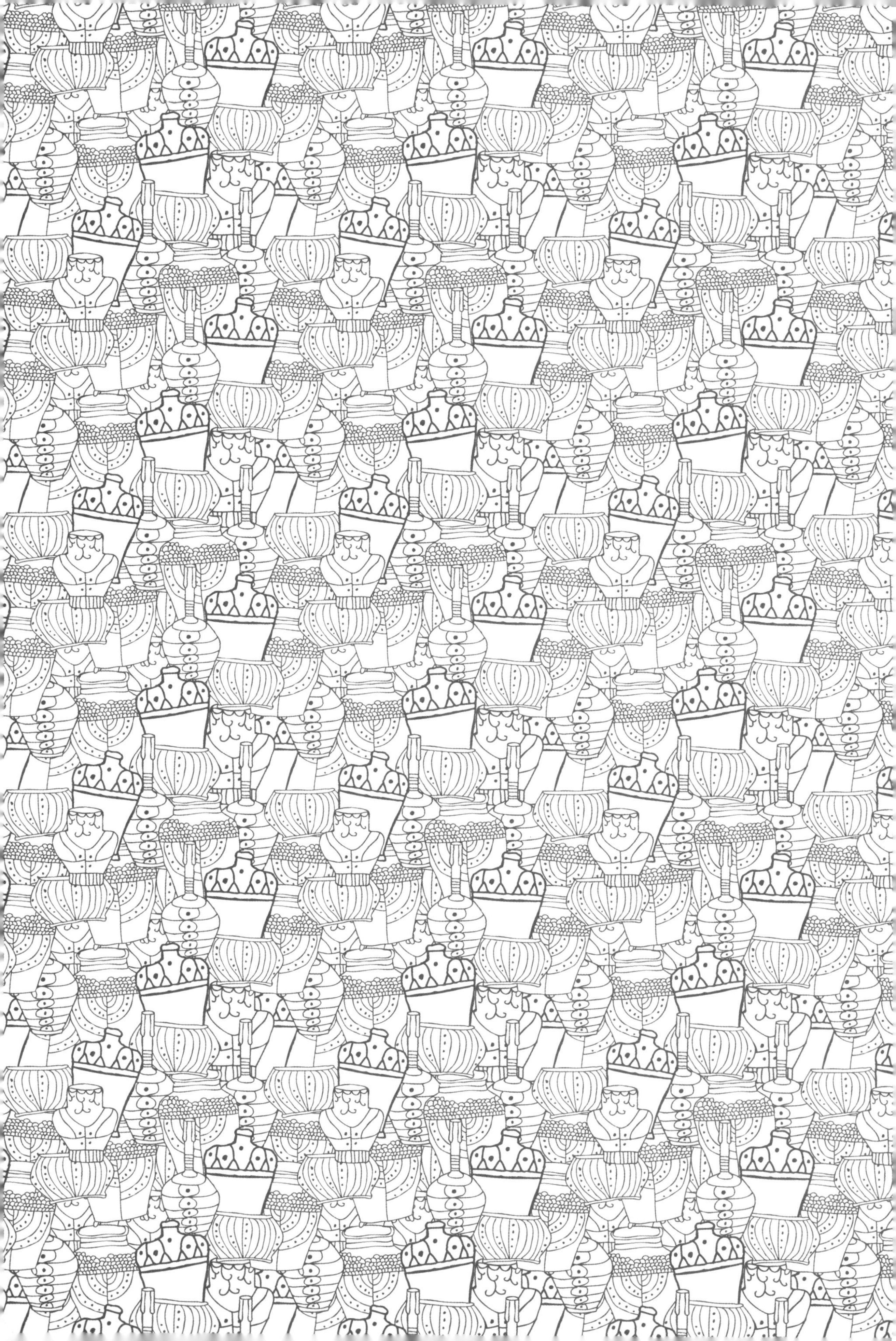

Wall Art • Concept

Wall Art • Concept •

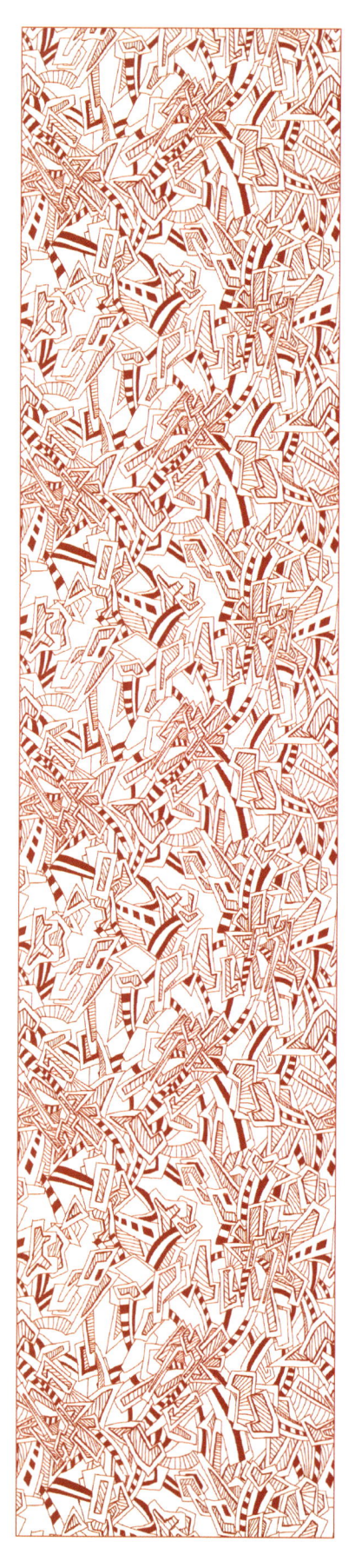

227

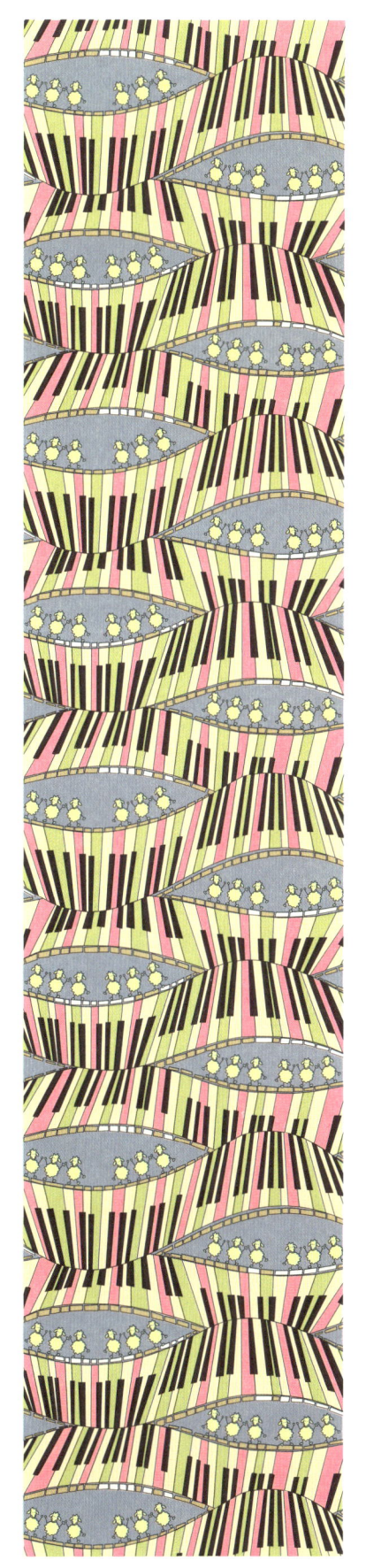

• Wall Art • Concept •

228

229

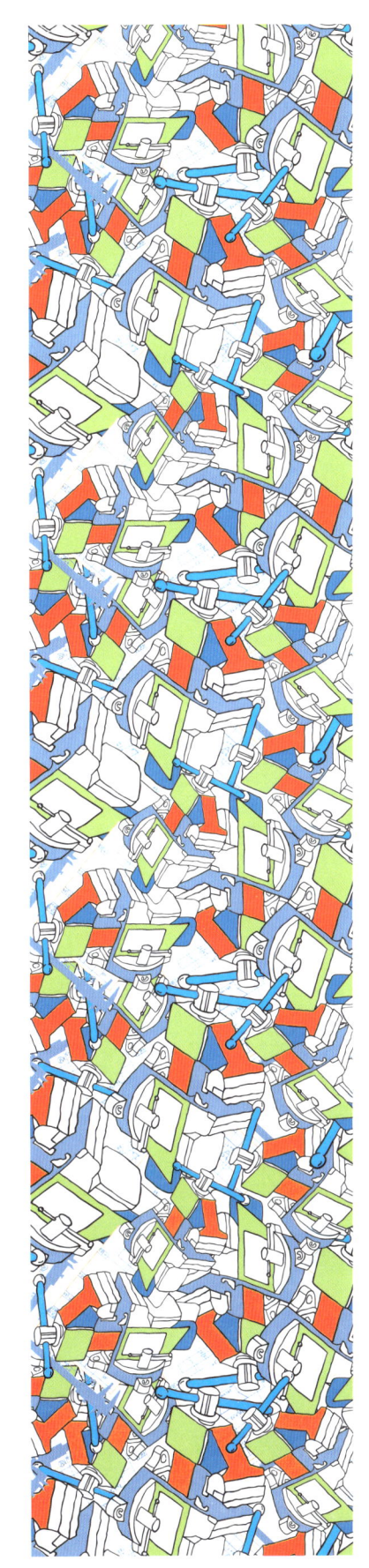

- Wall Art
- Concept

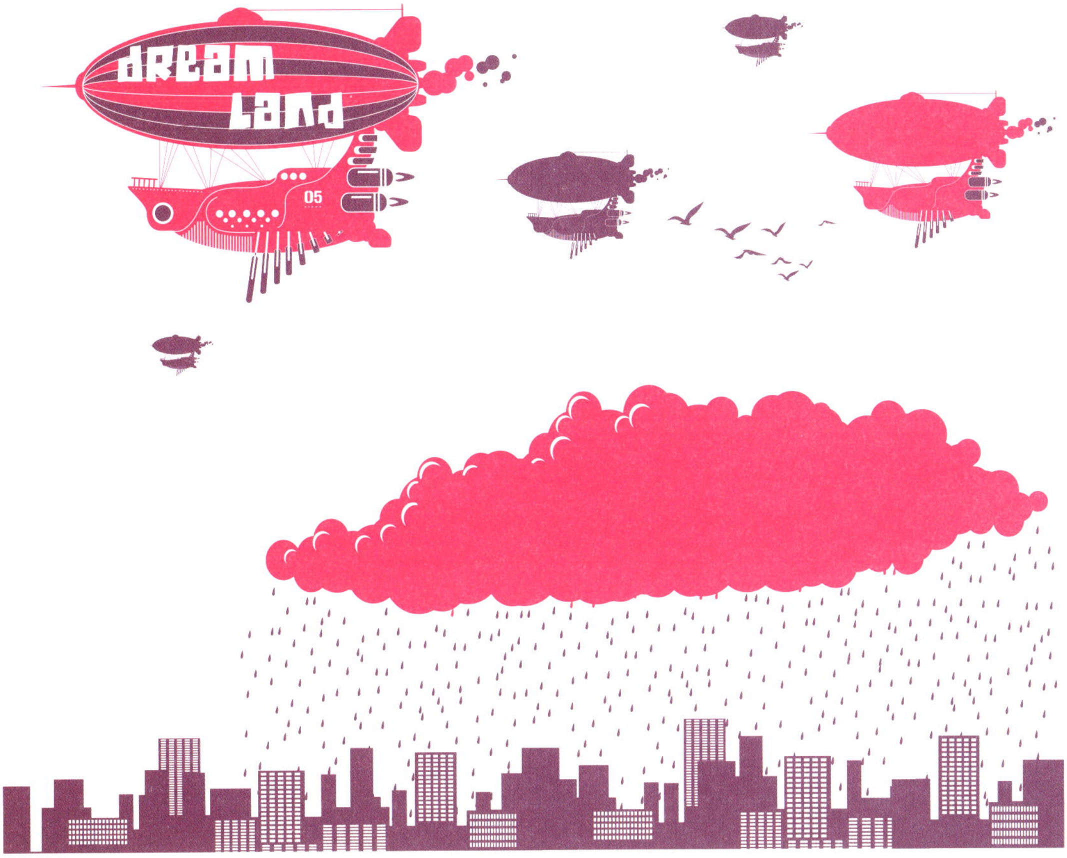
dream
land
05

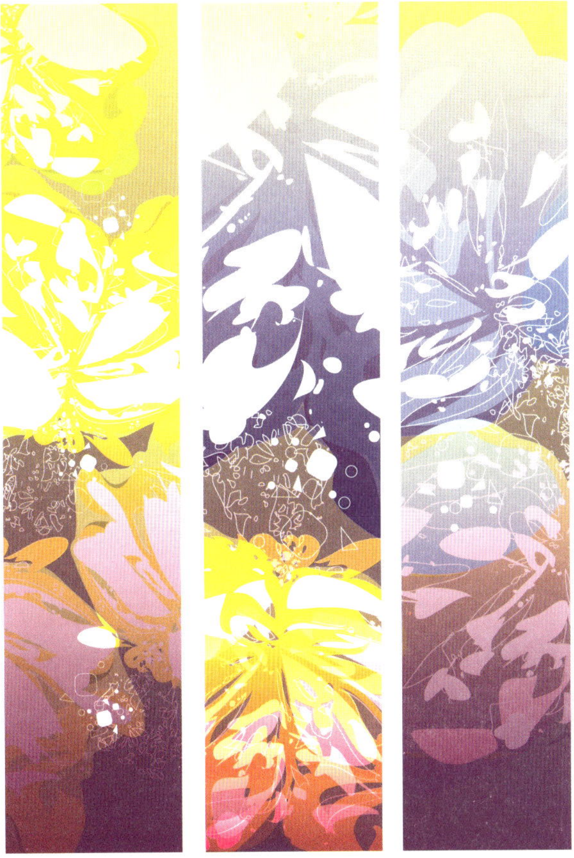

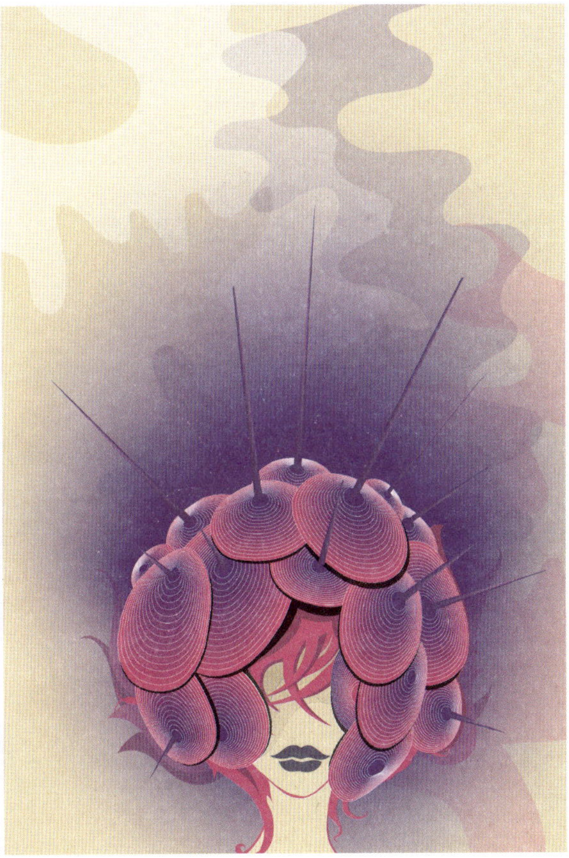

- Wall Art
- Concept

233

- Wall Art • Concept •

235

Wall Art • Concept •

236

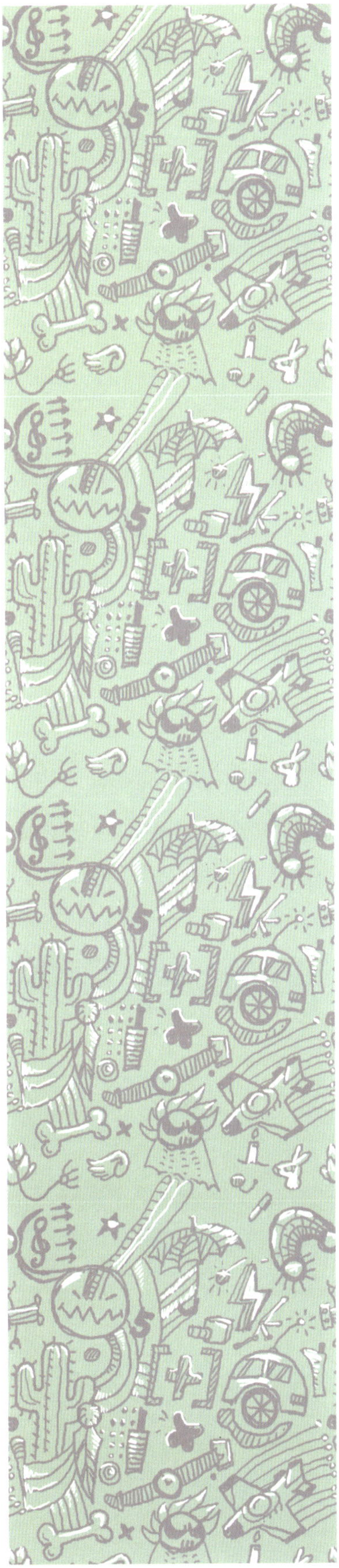

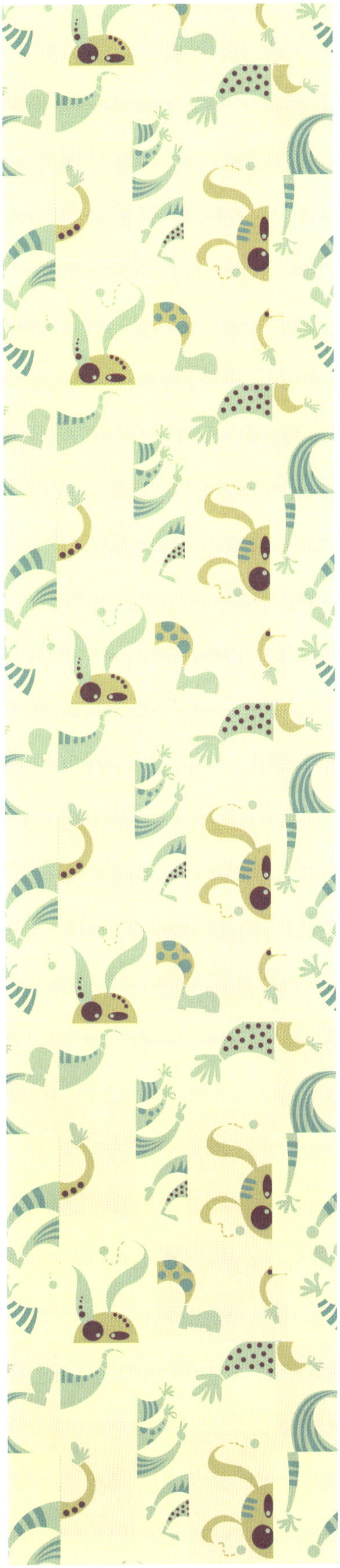

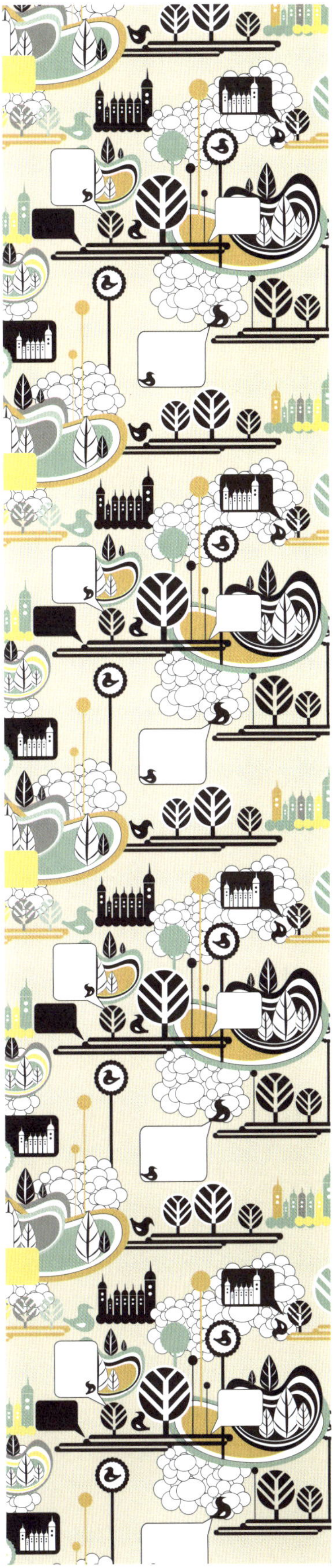

- Wall Art
- Concept

238

239

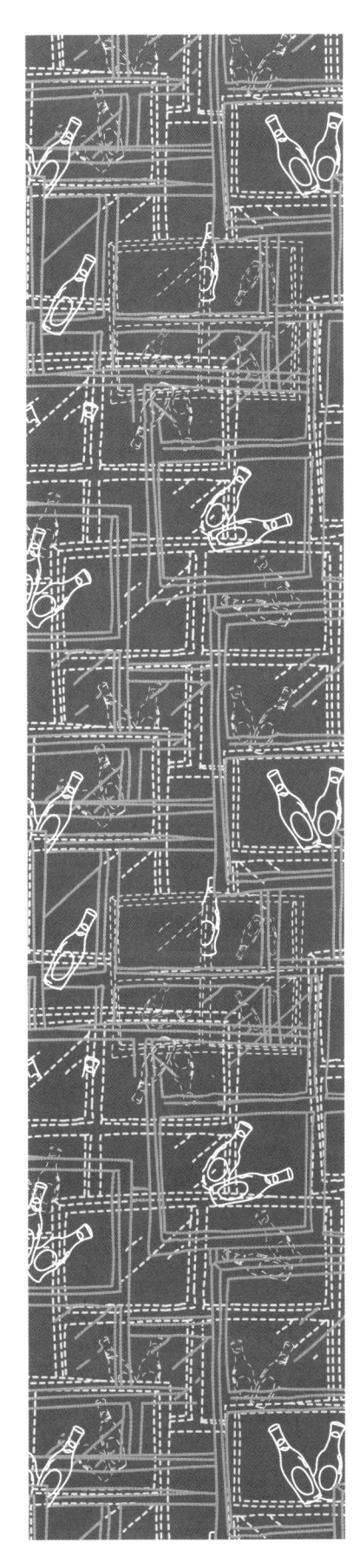

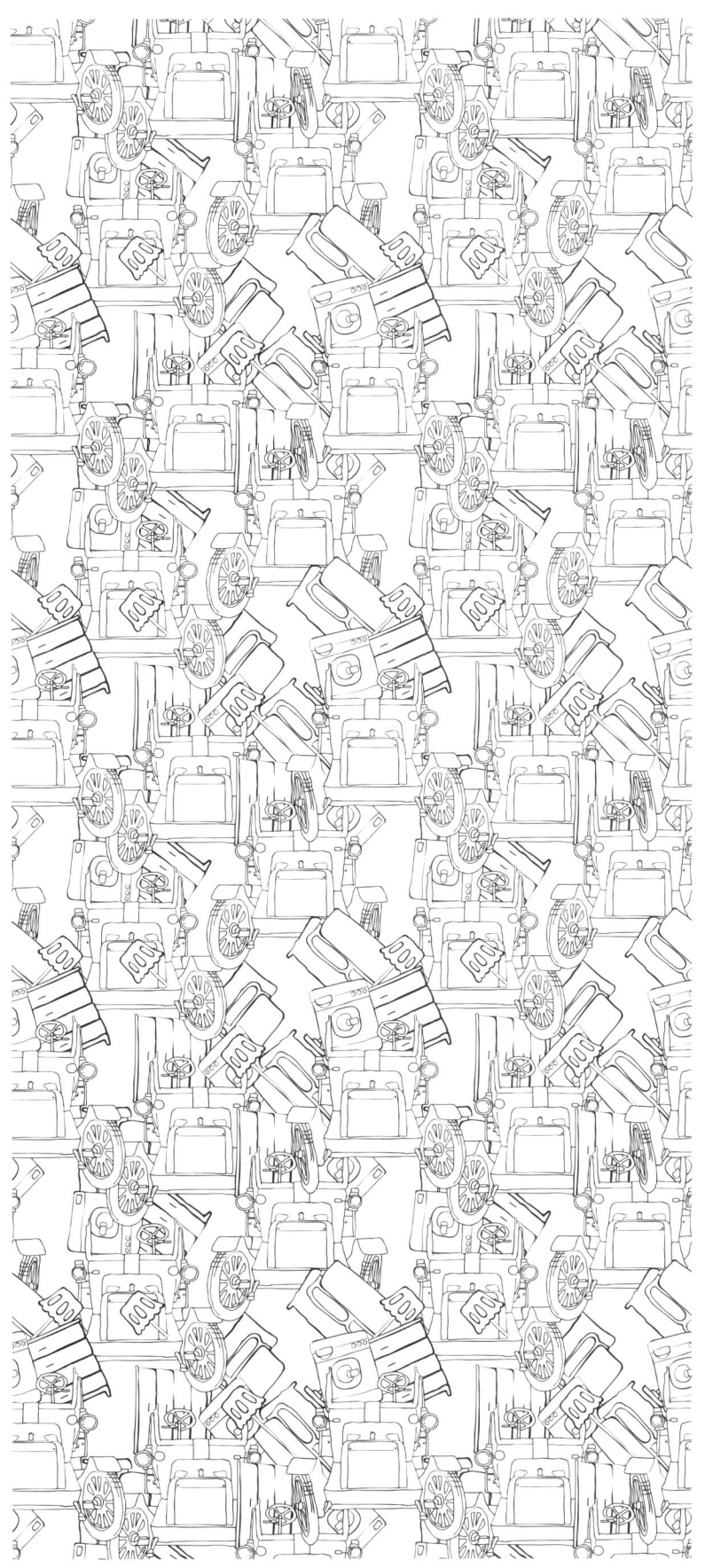

- Wall Art
- Concept

240

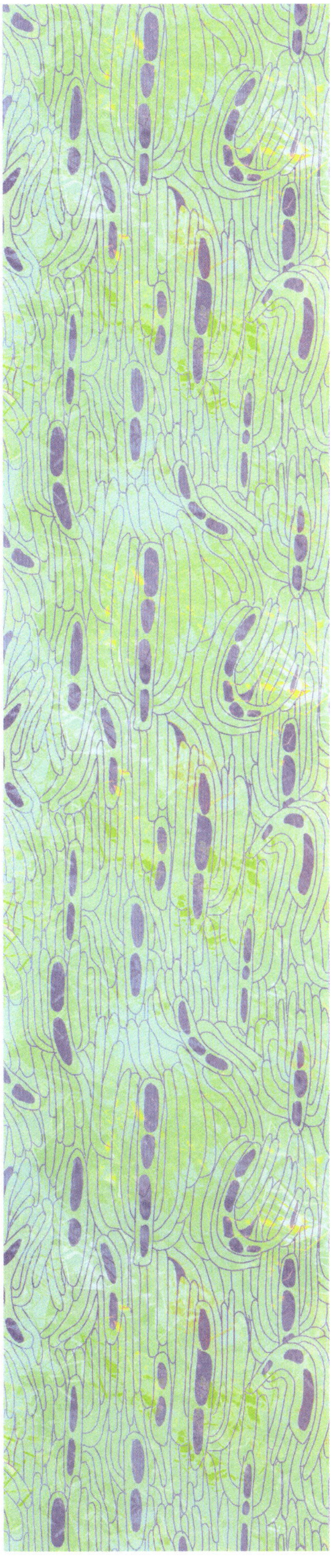

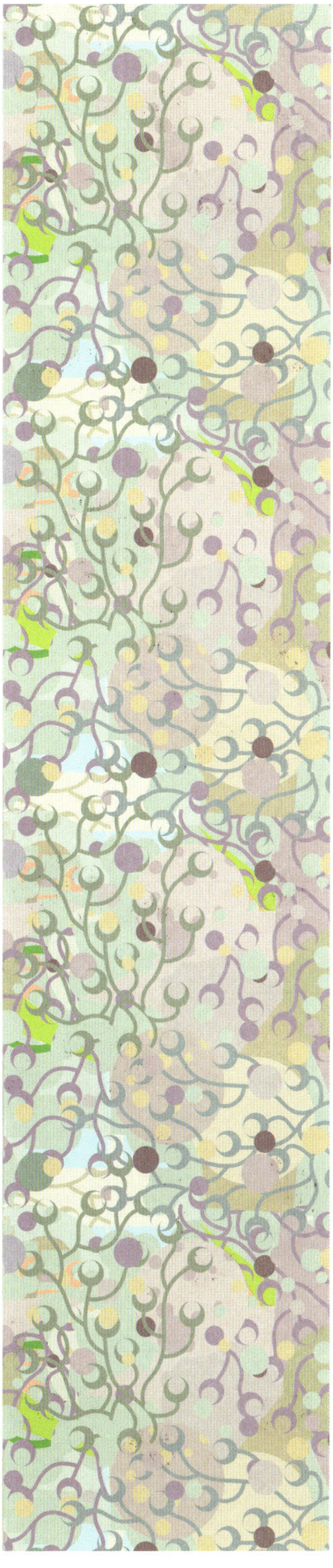

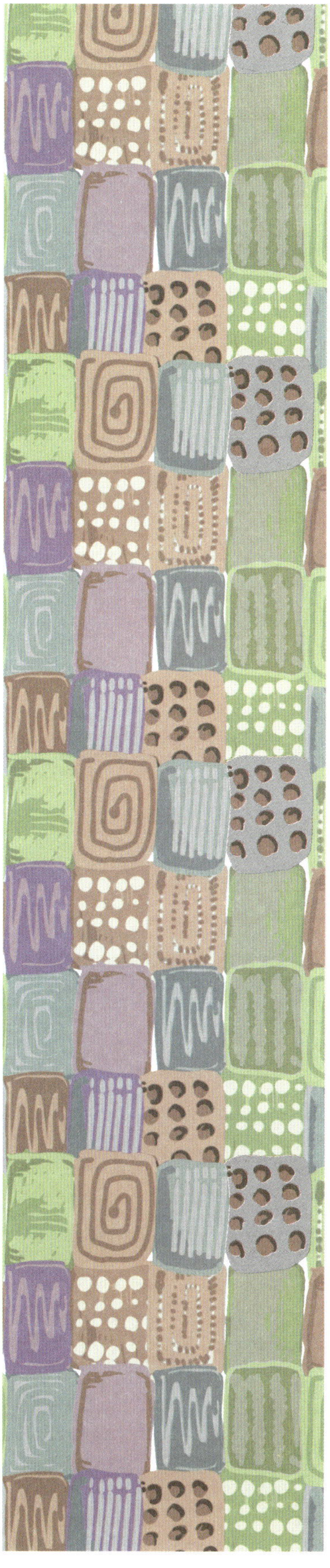

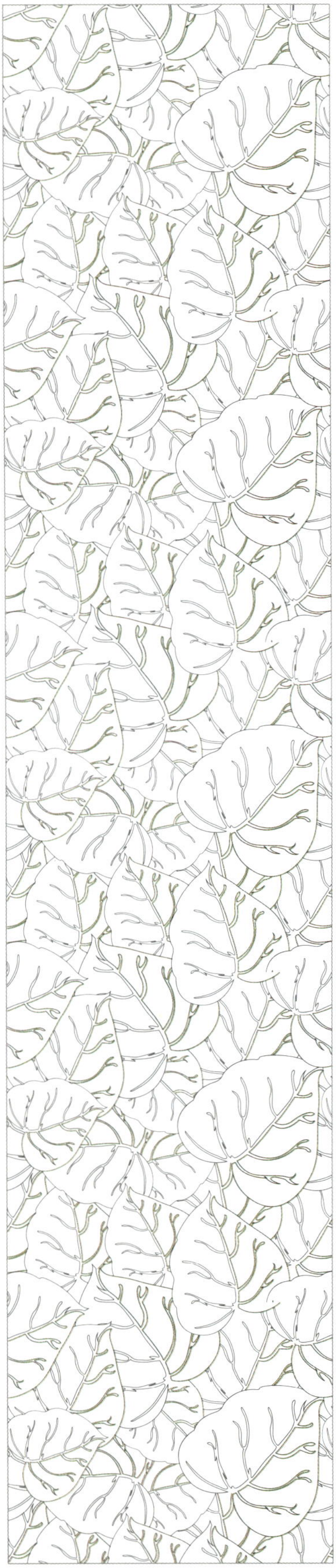

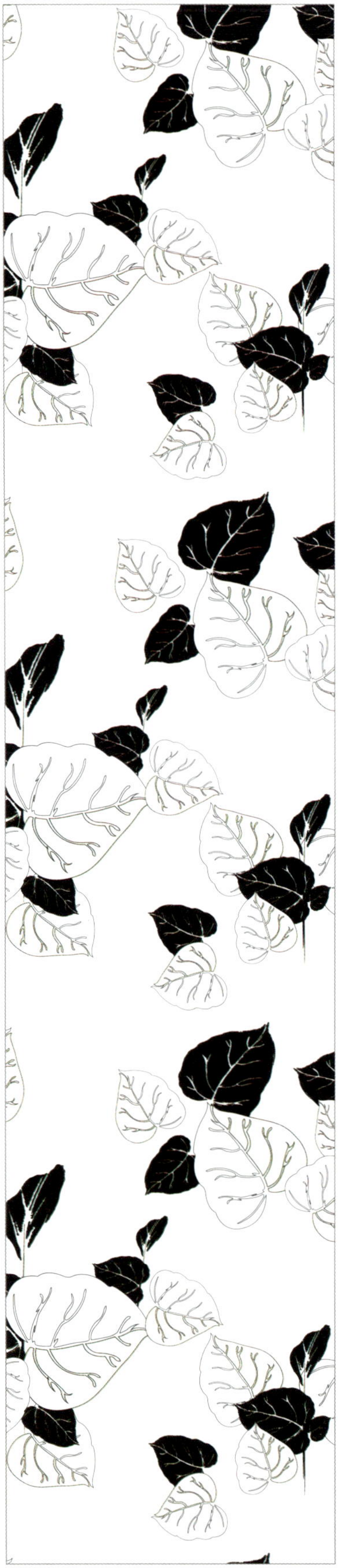

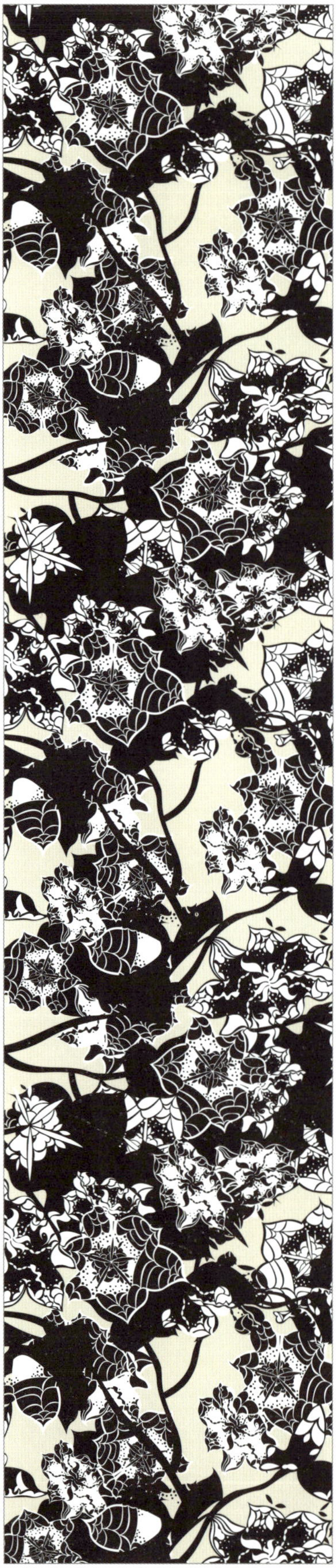

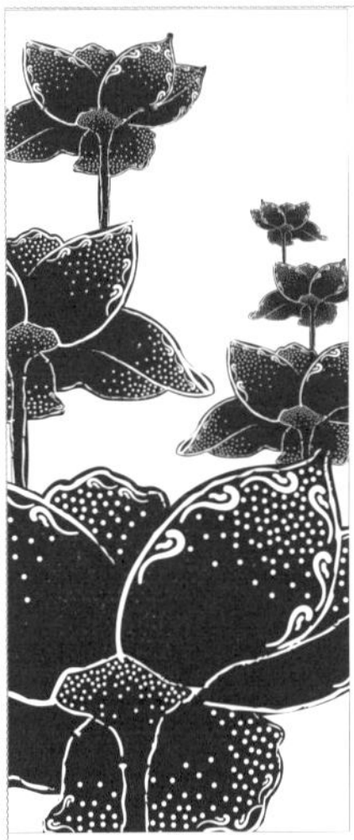
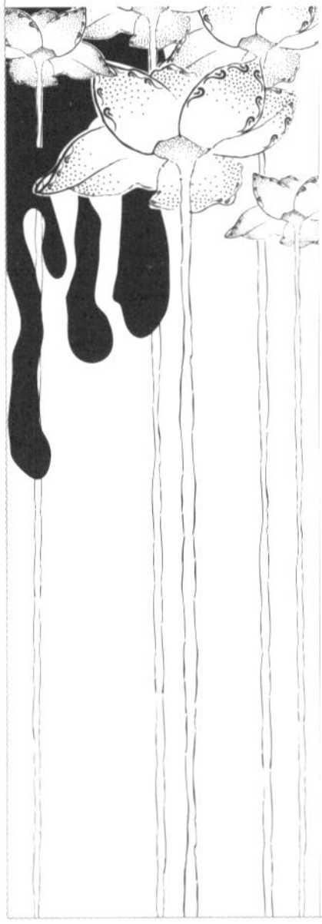
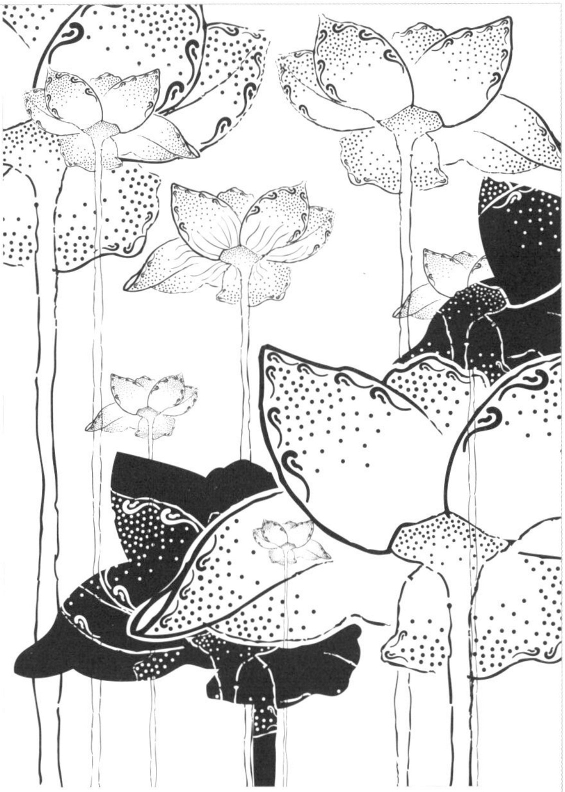
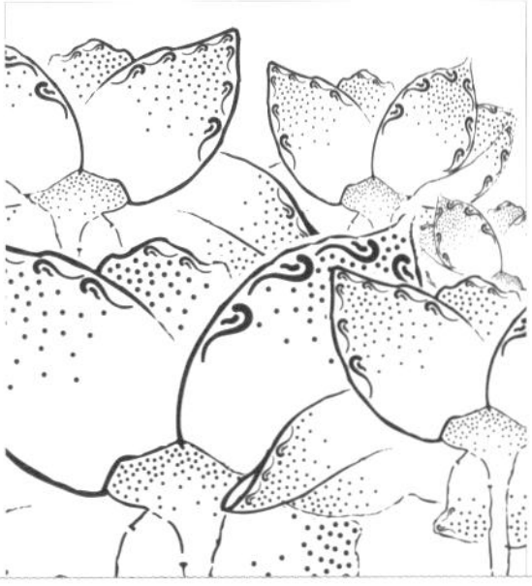
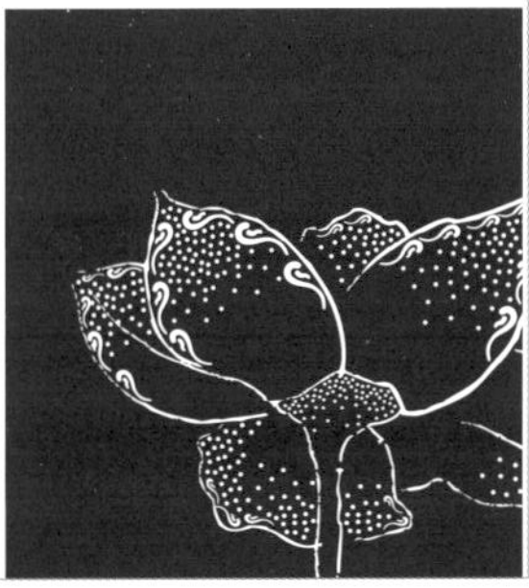
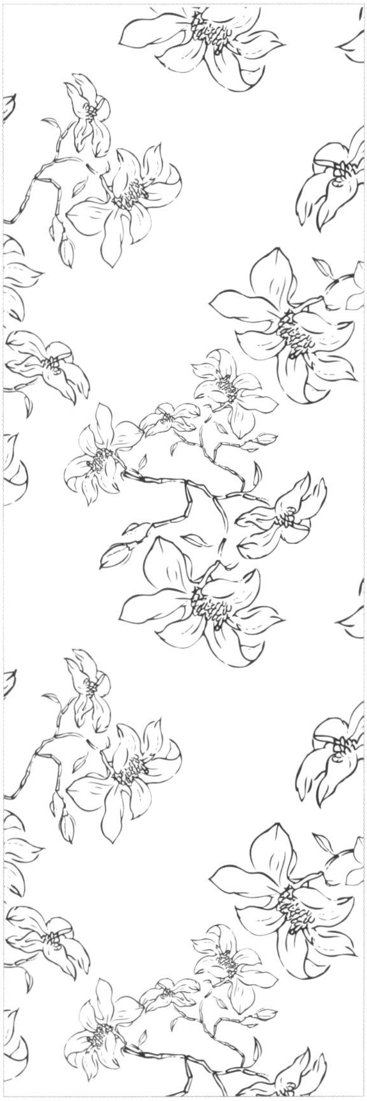
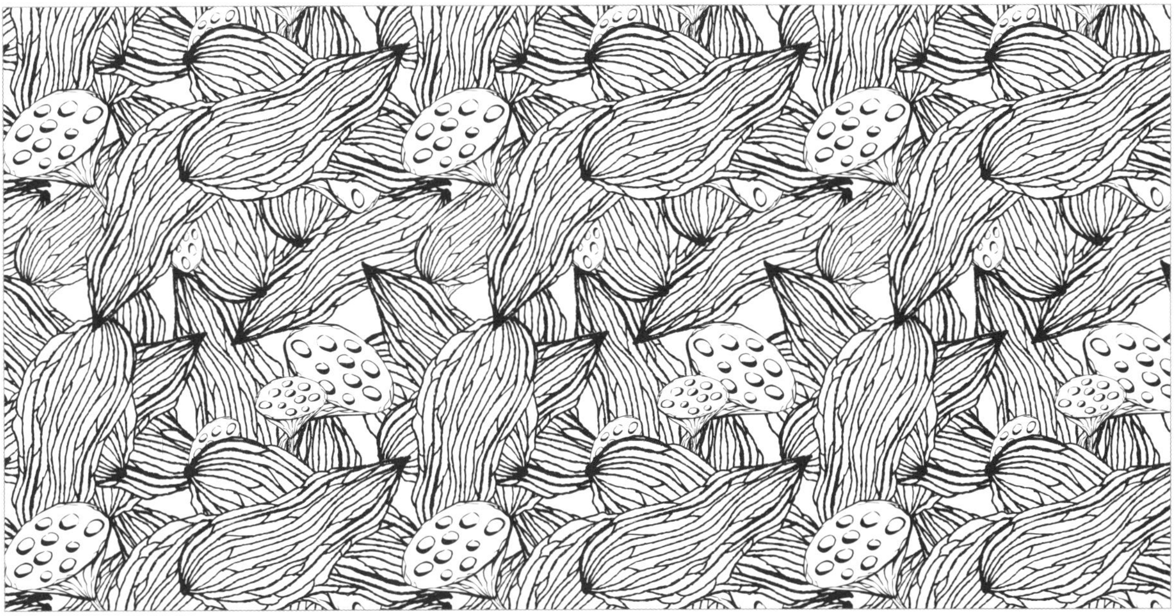

- Wall Art • Concept •

245

• Wall Art • Concept •

246

247

Wall Art • Concept •

249

- Wall Art
- Concept

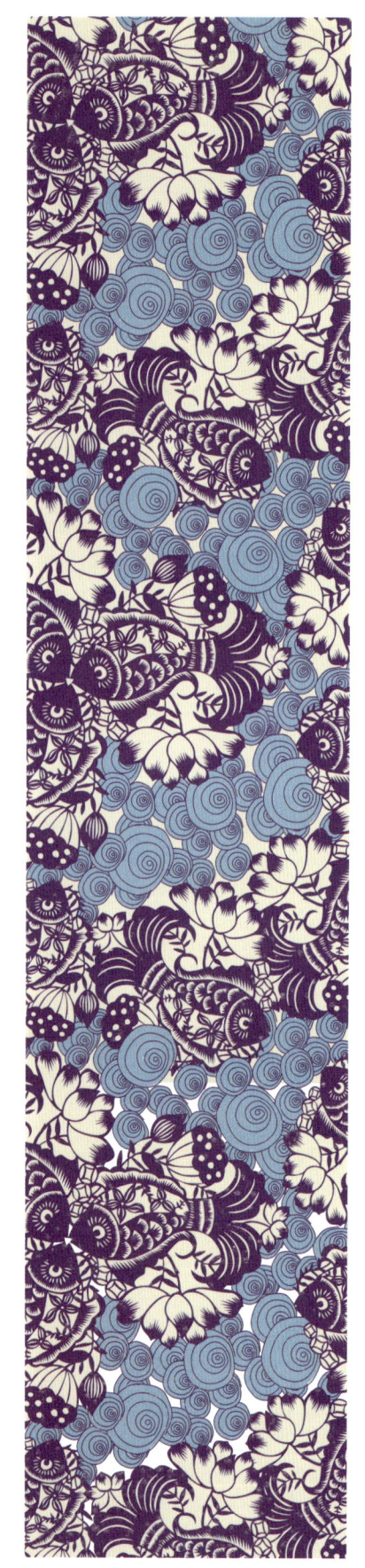

251

Abigail Borg

Add: UK
Tel: +44 (0) 7793033922
Web: www.abigailborg.co.uk
Email: contact@abigailborg.co.uk

Abigail is an illustrator and surface pattern designer with a love for the hand drawn approach to design. Her work varies in levels of intricacy and colour, being heavily influenced by traditional pattern design and illustration.

Having a great love for interior design and decoration, she has designed an award winning collection of wallpapers which combine traditional approaches to drawing and pattern with up to date digital printing, allowing for a touch of vintage inspired design to be applied in a modern setting.

Aimee Wilder

Add: Brooklyn, NY, USA
Tel: 646-691-6176
Web: www.aimeewilder.com
Email: info@aimeewilder.com

Born and raised in New York, Aimée spent her school holidays exploring the fashion showrooms where her parents both worked. From this early exposure to fashion trends and textiles, Aimée developed the foundation for her diverse interest in design and trends. She began working as a freelance graphic designer shortly after graduating from the School of The Art Institute of Chicago in 2001.

Aimée has also worked as an in-house designer for several firms including Dwell Studio, and Martha Stewart Living. She has designed for many well known brands, and is currently licensing her works for a wide range of products. In 2009 Vans featured three of her designs on 30 styles of shoes and fashion accessories. Aimee has also licensed two of her designs for a packages of novelty bandages currently available at many boutiques, most notably Urban Outfitters. Future collaborations will include products such as iphone covers, bedding, stationary, shower curtains, dishware, and vinyl toys.

Aimée draws her inspiration from contemporary graphic art and the design world. Influences include typography, logo design, illustration, textiles, urban toy design, rock poster art. Aimée's current projects include designs for home textiles and accessories, fashion and print.

Alexa Nice Interior Design

Add: Melbourne, Australia
Tel: +61408144083
Web: www.alexanice.com
Email: info@alexanice.com

Alexa Nice is founder and director of Alexa Nice Interior Design, specializing in high end hospitality design. Nice is an extremely passionate and highly talented designer with her unique style and attention to detail often described as intricately creative and divinely opulent. With a formal qualification in Bachelor of Built Environment majoring in interior design, Alexa has an impressive portfolio that spans hospitality, commercial, retail and high end residential, and has worked closely with one other creative director from the Film industry on various prestigious interiors in Brisbane, Australia.

Bigpen Studio

Add: Vilnius, Lithuania
Tel: +37062534099
Web: www.bigpen.ru
Email: funplastic@bigpen.ru, ammikhailov@gmail.com

Alexander Mikhaylov, the designer of Bigpen Studio, is a 29 year old Russian CG artist currently working as a freelancer. Now specializes in characters design, computer games, concept art, illustrations.

Branimir Sabljić

Add: 10000 Zagreb, Kriska 22, Croatia
Tel: +385 (0) 99 607 1979
Web: www.behance.net/BranimirSabljic
Email: branimir.sabljic@gmail.com

Branimir Sablji was born in Zagreb, Croatia, where he attended the high school for art and crafts - department for architecture and interior design, and presently attends the final year of the Faculty of design, University of Zagreb - Department for graphical design. He worked for six years as designer and art director in a design studio and an advertising agency before starting the career as a freelance artist and designer.

Branimir's work is heavily influenced by graffiti, which he started painting in his early adolescence. So far, he created more than twenty large murals, gradually developing his "true 3D" style. He also produced works in the fields of advertising, branding, exhibition design, interior design, painting, photo manipulation, print and web design, and organised several public graffiti-jam events for children and youth.

Brunella Giannangeli

Add: Madrid, Spain
Web: www.brugiannangeli.com
Email: info@brugiannangeli.com, b.giannangeli@gmail.com

Coming from a multidisciplinary design background and now settled in Madrid, Venezuelan-born textile & surface designer, Brunella Giannangeli, takes the world of patterns to another level by experimenting with different means. From fashion and interior textiles to wallpapers and stationery, her intention is to create timeless pieces that posses a defined and stylish visual identity while applying a strong structural sense.

Camelia Nedelcu

Add: Timisoara, Romania
Web: camelianedelcu.wordpress.com, camelianedelcu.com
vimeo.com/user1461198/videos
Email: camelianedelcu@gmail.com

Camelia Nedelcu is a 24 years old freelancer. In 2009 she finished the Arts University with a bachelor degree in photo-video. But still, she is trying to develop a wide platform of creativity, that's why her activity field is much larger. Her goal is to persevere in motion graphic.

Carol Rivello

Add: Santa Catarina, Brazil
Web: www.carolrivello.com
Email: carolrivello@gmail.com

Carol Rivello has a degree in Design, but she loves art direction and illustration as well. She's worked in Brazil and Italy, creating for clients such as SPFW, Mitsubishi Motors, Microsoft and Petrobras. Now she happily lives and works as a freelancer in Florianópolis, a pretty little island in the south of Brazil. Pigs, internet, music, movies, travelling and ice cream are her passions.

Dopludó Collective

Add: Moscow, Russia
Web: www.dopludo.com, www.be.net/dopludo/frame
Email: dopludo.info@gmail.com

Dopludó Collective was found in St. Petersburg in 2006. Word "Dopludó" comes from a phonetic transcription of French words "deux plus deux", which is "two plus two" in English. At the heart of the name of a creative trio lays the absurd mathematical formula "2+2=5", which has been proved several times and being a potential key to reconsider all mathematics from the beginning.

Dopludó teammates enjoy working with the images from magic fairy tales, folk elements, mystical and more or less abstract content, usually taking a position of looking at the world with the eyes of unsophisticated child, whose life is still a trip of discovering new miracles. In working with sense, main themes of collective's works are convention of all borders, prevalence of essence over existence, primacy of consciousness over a matter. Together they work on installations, objects, illustrations, interiors and public projects in cold Russia and Scandinavia.

D-Bend Design Studio

Add: Belgrade, Serbia
Web: www.d-bend.com
Email: office@d-bend.com

D-Bend is a Belgrade-based design studio founded by Vanja Vikalo and Mirko Lazarevic as a result of an idea born on a New Year's Eve 2007-2008.

D-Bend, mainly focuses on design for fashion and music industry, visual identity for bands and brands, motion graphics, logo and character design and design for print.

E-glue

Add: 3 rue de la Tour du Pin 69004 Lyon - France
Tel: +33 (0) 9 54 00 97 96
Email: info@e-glue.fr

Graduated from French Higher School of Decorative Arts, the E-glue team has founded in 2006 a creative studio specialized in design & communication for kids and launched their own products aimed at giving a contemporary view to the world of accessories & decors for kids.

Considering space as a blank page, E-glue brings illustration for kids to life with a range of contemporary graphic designs featuring favourites such as savanna, jungle, pirates, underwater world, train, robots, princesses, dinosaurs and many more! Offering a wide catalogue regularly enriched with new decorative stickers, E-glue proposes theme packs or single giant decals to adapt the to children's spaces.
E-glue wall decals are made in France from solid colour material that is laser cut (not printed) into shapes. Colours are much richer and the material is also very thin, so it lays beautifully on surfaces for a realistic look as if it were painted on.

Elizabeth Corkery

Add: 107 North 1st St Apt 1b, Brooklyn, NY 11211, USA
Tel: 917-238-8157
Web: www.elizabethcorkery.com
Email: elizabeth.corkery@gmail.com

Elizabeth is a native of Sydney, Australia. She received her BFA (Hons) in Printmaking from the College of Fine Arts, UNSW and continues her printmaking practice largely in the medium of silkscreen.

Elizabeth has an ongoing fascination with the notion of the multiple and where her works is placed in the growing intersection of fine art and design. Printmaking, at its heart is concerned with the creation of limited editions and Elizabeth enjoys inverting this idea by using printmaking to create what she called "unique multiples"; printed works created en masse where no two pieces are the same and can exist as individual works and also as wall coverings.

Estúdio Romeu & Julieta

Add: Rua Sao Manoel, 1197 - Sala 602, Ed. Oyster. Porto Alegre, Rio Grande do Sul, Brasil. CEP 90620-110
Tel: +55 65 3023-6255
Web: www.romeuejulieta.net
Email: atendimento@romeuejulieta.net

As a freelance illustrator and animator for more than four years, Jean Campos has accumulated experience and strength in his work, making it increasingly conceptual and open to new techniques. Today he heads the Estúdio Romeu & Juliet, which is a Partner and responsible for the whole of creation and direction of the illustrations and animations that the company develops. Romeu & Juliet is a milestone in his career, the realization of a dream. Having a studio with structure and support of care and planning of everything that is done are fantastic.

Good Wives and Warriors

Add: London, United Kingdom
Web: www.goodwivesandwarriors.co.uk
Email: hello@goodwivesandwarriors.co.uk

Good Wives and Warriors is the creative partnership between Becky Bolton and Louise Chappell, who met while studying painting at the Glasgow School of Art. Rebecca means "good wife" and Louise means "warrior", and together they create weird and wonderful illustrations and sprawling wall-paintings. They are currently based in London.

Katrin Olina

Add: Bergstadastraeti 7, 101 Reykjavik, Iceland
Web: www.katrin-olina.com
Email: info@katrin-olina.com

Born in Iceland, Katrin Olina studied Industrial Design at the E.S.D.I. in Paris before working in the European design studios of Philippe Starck (Paris) and Ross Lovegrove (London). Since then, she has worked predominantly as a graphic artist and illustrator in the realms of industrial design, fashion, interiors, print, and animation, as well as participating in several prominent museum and gallery exhibitions.

Olina has developed a rich visual language that serves as a vivid interface between reality and the subconscious mind. Much of her work contains natural elements that combine the fairytale and the sublime, consisting of lush landscapes inhabited by real and fictional creatures, as well as characters tied to her own personal history.

Her most recent major project is Cristal Bar in Hong Kong, where her dream-like drawings cover every interior surface, enabling a new level of interactivity in three-dimensional space. Cristal Bar has won numerous international awards, including the Forum Aid Awards in Stockholm, SEGD merit prize in San Diego and the DV culture prize in Iceland 2009.

Through her own company, Katrin Olina Ltd., she has fabricated a range of limited edition products—including silk scarves, hand painted porcelain products, fashion accessories, snowboards and helmets and bags.

Kingdrips

Add: Kingdrips GbR, Wohlwillstr. 27, 20359 Hamburg, Germany
Tel: +49 (0) 40 530 22 655
Web: www.kingdrips.com
Email: info@kingdrips.com

Kingdrips is a multidisciplinary design studio based in Hamburg, Germany.

The aesthetic influences range from graffiti and urban scenes to design and fine arts. As they juggle with different individual styles, they juggle with the boundaries between fine arts and commercially interesting works: in their eyes, it is a smooth transition as long as they don't come into conflict with their creative and artistic freedom.

It's all about Friendship and the dream to live like they like to – to work and have fun doing it!

LAB261

Add: KFKS: Anastasia Akulinina, NY/Russia.
SFHD: Anna Novikova, Russia
Email: lab261@gmail.com
KFKS: kaerfkrahs@gmail.com
SFHD: skyfirehead@gmail.com
Web: www.kaerfkrahs.com, www.behance.net/skyfirehead

LAB261 is an art group since 2006,consisting of two people: KFKS & SFHD.

LeighLeigh

Add: The Midlands, United Kingdom
Tel: 0116 254 5269, 0792 040 4508
Web: www.leighleigh.com
Email: design@leighleigh.com

Producing creative graphics and illustrations for design studios, local and national businesses, charities and monthly magazines since 2005.

An outstanding creative portfolio details Leigh's particular attention to detail across many design fields. A strong skill set of Leigh's rests in print design including brochures, Identity, books, magazines, pamphlets, leaflets, editorial, posters, annual reports, bespoke designs and many more. He has exceptionally strong typographic skills and has created his own typefaces in the past when an off-the-shelf typeface just wouldn't do it.

Malene Landgreen

Add: ML Office, Læderstræde 15,
DK-1201 Copenhagen, Denmark;
ML Studio, Schinkelstrasse 9B, DE- 12047 Berlin, Germany
Web: www.malenelandgreen.dk
Email: info@malenelandgreen.dk

Ms Malene Landgreen, a visual Artist, lives and works in Copenhagen and Berlin.

Malene Landgreen's work represents an unlikely merger between on the one hand a Scandinavian abstract colour field painting of the 50's and on the other hand American post-war abstraction, pop-art included.

However, first and foremost Malene Landgreen is a painter who in her work is exploring the psychological, emotional, cognitive and material potentialities of colour and space on two-dimensional surfaces. She works mostly in large scales, either on big canvases or directly on walls. The combination of rigor and openness, compositional delicacy and serial standardization, is characteristic of her working method which also involves thorough considerations on the handling of paint, the texture, the stroke, and the nuance. The resulting works are strikingly sensual and playful in their combination of colours, extremely complex in terms their visual communication and spatially intriguing.

Miss Led

Add: London, United Kingdom
Tel: +44 (0) 7888894333
Web: www.missled.co.uk
Email: mail@missled.co.uk

Award winning live painter and illustrator both in London and Europe, Joanna Henly is barely in her 2nd year of working under the guise of Miss Led. In this time she has managed to amass a lucrative body of work with a high profile clientele.

From painting live, a window for Selfridges and large-scale illustration work for Reebok and Diesel to painting bespoke interior pieces for celebrities and Brompton Rd boutiques. Led has created her distinctively playful, flirtatious and diverse styles on many surfaces in a plethora of mediums. Her illustrations have been commissioned; her artwork featured and published in magazines and newspapers nationwide. With a string of group shows under her belt she plans for a solo exhibition next year.

Miss Lee Design

Add: Ha'amoraim st. Tel Aviv Israel
Tel: +972-54-3456798
Web: www.missleedesign.com
Email: info@missleedesign.com

Miss Lee Design is a young, innovative studio for interior design and brand-image which focuses on business and commercial spaces. In order to build a cohesive language, the studio team looks at the brand through the consumers' eyes and integrate themselves into the development of it at its concept phase, while thoroughly researching its needs and identity.

The studio believes there is a direct correlation between the design of a space and the brands image. The studio strives to create consistency and uniformity between the space, the brand and its graphics; an advantage that gives the brand a strong and reliable image.

The customers experience starts at the stage where they meet the graphic image of a business: the logo, business cards, website, etc. The experience is completed when the customer reaches the designed space. The graphic language they have come to know is visually expressed in a three dimensional, real space. The visual expression is manifested in the architecture, the space plan, choice of materials, details, lighting, colours, furniture and the entire design element that give the space its identity and influences the users senses.

Nawer

Add: Artde7 Inside Design Krakow
Tel: +48 604411636
Web: www.artde7.com, www.behance.net/nawer
Email: madnaw1@o2.pl

Architect, designer, street artist, graduate of Architecture and Urbanism program in Krakow. Has been involved with street art since the mid 90's. In 2003, began to devote time between painting and freelancing in interior design. Created Artde7 Studio in 2006, with a focus on interior and graphic design, along with scenography.

Creativity stems toward isometric graphics as extant of public and functional spaces. Interior spatiality is described as a blend of objects within space, while painting by perspective and axonometry using aerosol as a main medium. The combination of these two approaches allows a fresh take on the design of arrangement and creativity of an interior space. As his own style evolves, the goal is to always strive forward in an effort to connect painting with architecture.

Neosbrand

Add: Recinto interior Zona Franca. Edif. Melkart, nº25 Andalucía, Spain
Tel: +34 956 07 00 60
Web: www.neosbrand.com
Email: info@neosbrand.com

We are a study of graphical design, publicity and branding, formed by a group of young graphic designers, copywriters and advertisers that love communication.

We like to create and update brands in a world in continuous motion, making communication actions that help to protect and guard them, managing to connect with their target public.

Olefir Zoya

Add: 46008 Ternopil, Ukraine, Pidlisna St. 48
Tel: +380 352 067 3541928
Email: olefirdesign@gmail.com

Olefir Zoya is a designer from Ukraine, who specializes in creating interior design and focuses on decorative walls (pannos) creation. Each project is always a unique piece of art which is made in one specimen and is never repeated again. Surrounding a human in daily life, every object must provide emotions, beauty and aesthetic pleasure.

Osborne & Little

Add: Riverside House, 26 Osiers Road, London SW18 1NH
Tel: +44 (0)20 8812 3000, +44 (0)20 8812 3030
Fax: +44 (0)20 8877 7500
Email: Enquiries: oandl@osborneandlittle.com
Export enquiries: exports@osborneandlittle.com

Osborne & Little are leading fabric and wallpaper designers. They are also distributors of Nina Campbell, Liberty Furnishings, Lorca and Michael Reeves Furniture.

Patric Sandri

Add: Zurich, Switzerland, dietenrainweg 3, ch-8610 uster
Tel: +41(0)765922540
Web: www.patricsandri.com, patricsandri-illustration.blogspot.com
Email: info@patricsandri.com

As a designer, Patric Sandri is a Zurich based freelance illustrator who has worked for newspapers locally, nationally and internationally.

Clients have included DU magazine, Star Alliance, Hochparterre Magazine (CH), greenpeace (CH) Sonntagszeitung (CH), BAZ (Baslerzeitung) (CH), Rote Fabrik (CH), WOZ (CH), Schweizer Beobachter (CH), Raffinnerie (CH), novo-magazin (d), every weekend magazine (indonesia), Skinnymagazine (UK), HSLU (CH) and Truce (CH). He creates conceptual and stylized images. He is available for commercial advertising projects, paintings, editorials, posters, CDs, visual essays, reportages and storyboard work.

Reaktor Lab

Add: Libertad 1840-A, C.P. 44160. Guadalajara, Jalisco
Tel: +52(33) 3070 1443
Web: www.reaktorlab.com, www.behance.net/reaktorlab
Email: contacto@reaktorlab.com

Reaktor is the human condition that empowers you to think by yourself and transcend. It's one that raises his voice and never gives up. It's not following trends, but having the power to create them and modifying what surrounds you. It's having a solid argument and an unbreakable will.

Reaktor is to live maximizing your own essence. Reaktor is the beginning; it's the motor that keeps everything running. It's being the cause that triggers consequences. Reaktor is one that has no fear of change. Reaktor is change; it's generating reactions. At the lab, under Jorge Aguilar's supervision, we find ourselves in a continuous visual exploration, constantly bold and always curious. As a result, we find fresh, innovating solutions that endure and are high valued.

The lab is the idea-generating nucleus, constantly changing; it's where arts, graphics, and motion graphics merge with creativity and communication. Altogether, these elements set the essence of each project free, unleashing their reaction potential.

ROW Studio

Add: Palmas 1145 Lomas de Chapultepec C.P. 11000, México, Distrito Federal, Mexico
Tel: +52(55)47539565
Web: www.rowarch.com
Email: info@rowarch.com

ROW Studio is an architecture and design firm founded by Álvaro Hernández Felix and Alfonso Maldonado Ochoa in 2005.

Its name derives from the term used in economy to refer to global phenomena (ROW: Rest of the World), as a critical standpoint against the clichés of Mexican architecture and the need to generate an international discourse both in processes and proposals departing from a multidisciplinary approach. At the same time it addresses the need of expanding the field study and influence from architecture to other disciplines such as sociology, psychology, economy, marketing, etc.

RR Army Studio

Add: RRARMY Studio Barcelona, Camí Del Gual S. N., 08187 Barcelona, Spain
Tel: (+34) 662 446 007
Web: www.rrarmy.com
Email: contact@rrarmy.com

RRARMY is the studio of the Romero brothers; Ibie & Edjinn. "We are dedicated to graphic design, illustration and art direction, among other things."

Sandy Canvas

Add: 969 Richards Street, Suite 1908, Vancouver, BC V6B 1A8, Canada
Web: www.sandycanvas.com
Email: sandra@sandycanvas.com

As the founder of Sandy Canvas, Sandy is an illustrator and photographer. Her knowledge, experience and technical skills did not happen over night.

It has taken many years to develop her creative vision, capturing memory through an exploration of nature's beautiful geometric proportions. In elementary school, she was given her first film camera and was taught the basic principles involved in taking a photograph. As an artistic child, she used these photos to create her artwork, scrapbooks, cards and colleges, each rewarding her with memories that have defined her life.

Skills Division

Add: Belgrade, Serbia
Tel: (+381) 11 299 2703

Web: www.skillsdivision.com, www.facebook.com/skillsdivision
Email: kontakt@skillsdivision.com

Skills Division is a group of visual artists, currently based in Belgrade, Serbia. Their works are focused on set / stage design, stand design, interiors, exteriors, store windows, costumes, graphic design. Besides designers their team consists of sculptors, painters and model makers that are leading a workshop where ideas of creative team are instantly brought into reality.

Staynice

Add: Keizerstraat 96, 4811 HL Breda, The Netherlands
Tel: 003176-5322553
Web: www.staynice.nl
Email: staynice@staynice.nl

Staynice are two brothers, Rob and Barry van Dijck.

In 2007 they started their company, after graduating from AKV St.Joost, academy of fine arts in Breda, Netherlands. Their characteristic work had drawn a lot of attention at the academy.

They have both been nominated for the 'St.Joost penning', an award for most promising student. As a result of that nomination, they won a workspace for one year at artist space and gallery KOP in Breda. From that moment, Staynice is official. Their motive is to leave something personal behind, something which lasts. Ever since they were young, we have felt drawn to this. The need for it has only become stronger.

They worked among others for the Graphic Design Museum in Breda, Mascotte rolling papers, Vodafone, Van Gils clothing company, KOP, AKV St.Joost, Royal GMF GOUDA, Royal Broese en Peereboom, G2 Amsterdam, Mezz, Shop Around!, Playgrounds festival, Breda Barst festival, city of Breda, Vodafone, Club Trouw and 013.

Studio Lisa Bengtsson AB

Add: Atlasgatan 14, 113 20 Stockholm, Sweden
Tel: +46 (0) 70 57 99 345
Web: www.lisabengtsson.se
Email: Kontakt@lisabengtsson.se

After graduating from Bergh, Lisa decided to start her own business with her own design. In her business, she work primarily with pattern design, graphic design and illustrations. The inspiration comes from people and her own stories. For Lisa, it is important to communicate her own values and feelings. She communicates through images, colour, shape, pattern and typography to express messages or feelings to other people.

Tim Bjørn Design Studio

Add: Thurøvej 3, 2th, 2000 Frederiksberg, Copenhagen, Denmark
Tel: (+45) 2077 4692
Web: madebytim.com
Email: info@madebytim.com

Tim Bjørn, graphic designer. Situated in, calm and collected, Copenhagen, Denmark. This is the place where all work is done, these days, and inspiration is all around. Growing up in rural Denmark Tim loved drawing and painting, as many children do. But Tim might have loved it just a little bit more than your average kid. Turning to music at a teen age, Tim forgot about his crayons, and learned about the guitar and the many joys of music. This love has not died, but now takes a backseat to the graphic design.

Artistically and professionally Tim has started out without any formal education. As Tim moved to Copenhagen he was reintroduced to the world of design and art by friends, and it lit a spark in him. From this point there was no turning back and the career as a graphic designer started, fueled only by talent. After 4 years of disciplined training and hard work in a design studio, Tim was ready to fly solo, and now has the Tim Bjørn design studio.

Trapped in Suburbia

Add: De Caballero Fabriek, Saturnusstraat 60 Unit 81, 2516 AH Den Haag, the Netherland
Tel: 070 389 0858, Fax: 070 383 4823
Web: www.trappedinsuburbia.nl

Good design, tells a story, makes you smile, let's you play, is an experience and surprises you... They enjoy working at the cutting edge, challenging themselves and those around us, looking further than the length of our nose. They create conceptually and strategically strong projects with clear, clever designs and solutions. They think before they act, but they act before they talk.

Undoboy

Add: 1621 Zamia Avenue, Boulder, CO 80304, U.S.
Web: www.undoboy.com
Email: contact@undoboy.com

Undoboy is a design studio that embraces with a simple philosophy "design brings happiness". The works include brand identity design, editorial design, interactive design, character design, packaging design, toy design, motion graphics, and illustration.

Urszula Bogucka

Add: ul. Kotlarska 18 / 24, 31-539, Cracow, Poland
Web: www.ulab.pl; Portfolio: www.coroflot.com/public/individual_search_results.asp?keywords=urszula bogucka
Email: urszula.bogucka@gmail.com

Graphic Designer/Illustrator interested in exploring freelance opportunities or collaborations. She has her hands in quite a few areas, from illustrating, to identity design. Her skill set is diverse with concentration on layout and typography. She is living and working in Cracow, Poland. Her initial inspiration is always the client. A good brief inspires her and gets her thinking about the possibilities.

She has won some awards, such as "2009 Third Prize" in the poster competition Polish Diplomacy in Switzerland, "2007 First Prize" in the poster competition Contemporary Theatre in Warsaw, "2007 mention" in the competition Wall Paper Design Contest mediolan and "2007 mention" in the 2nd international Competition anti aids.

UXUS

Add: Keizersgracht 174, 1016 DW Amsterdam, Netherlands
Tel: +31 20 623 3114; Fax: +31 20 421 7669
Web: www.uxusdesign.com
Email: info@uxusdesign.com

Founded in Amsterdam in 2003, UXUS is an independent award wining design consultancy specializing in strategic design solutions for Retail, Communication, Hospitality, Architecture and Interiors.

UXUS creates "Brand Poetry", fusing together art and design, and creating new brand experiences for its clients worldwide. They define "Brand Poetry" as an artistic solution for commercial needs.

Artistic solutions target emotions; emotions connect people in a meaningful way. Design gives function, art gives meaning, and poetry expresses the essence.

Vêro Escalante

Add: Buenos Aires, Argentina
Web: www.behance.net/veroescalante
Email: vero.bee@gmail.com

Born in 1985 in a small town in Salta in northern Argentina, Vero Escalante is an illustrator and textile designer. Today she works and lives in Buenos Aires, Argentina. Part of her job is to think in concepts, looking for innovative aesthetic solutions, and always do everything with love.

Victor Sandoval

Add: Mexico
Tel: office (664) 608.01.00, movil (664) 196.69.24
Web: myspace.com/atomikamelancolica, facebook.com/victor sandoval, behance.net/atomicamelancolica
Email: atomicamelancolica@yahoo.com

Victor Sandoval, is a graphic designer/artist with a 20 years experience in the design and elaboration of artistic and comercial murals for any and every kind of space and ambience, working in restaurants, bars and night clubs, also in office buildings and hotels, and in private homes, also in film and tv commercials in mexico and abroad.

Wendy Plovmand

Add: London, UK; Copenhagen, Denmark
Tel: +44 (0) 7551 599 596, Uk, +(45) 2670 7452, DK
Web: www.wendyplovmand.com, www.centralillustration.com
Email: mail@wendyplovmand.com, info@centralillustration.com

Wendy Plovmand was born in Denmark currently residing in Copenhagen and London. Wendy works with both commercial projects and contemporary art. Her work bursts with energy and originality and is as much playful as it is edgy and lyrical. Her clients include Selfridges, GUESS, Organic Pharmacy, Nylon, Red Cross and the Guardian and she has exhibited in London, Copenhagen, Berlin, Tokyo and NYC.

woozy

Address: Flat 9 Park View House, Hurst Street, London SE24 0EQ
Tel: 0044 (0) 2072748943
Web: www.woozystore.com, www.woozydesign.com
Email: info@woozystore.com

Profile: Woozy born from the mind of two creative designers, specialising in illustration, decorative graphics and concept design.

The collection is totally conceptualized designed and produced by us to offer a product that is 100% handmade. Our aim is to create and stimulate spaces using brand new techniques as a fresh, innovative, alternative to traditional decoration.

York Wall-coverings

Add: 750 Linden Avenue, York, PA 17405-5166, USA
Tel: 717-846-4456
Web: www.yorkwall.com

America's oldest and largest wallpaper manufacturer, York has been making wall-coverings since 1895 in its original location in Pennsylvania's Susquehanna Valley. A well-loved fixture in the York, PA community, the company continues to thrive and grow as an American manufacturer creating some of the world's favorite wall-covering brands.

WALL ART: WALL PAPER / PAINTING / DECORATION / STICKER
COPYRIGHT © 2011 DOPRESS BOOKS

First published 2011 by
Dopress Books
No 85-3, Huanghe South Street,
110031 Shenyang, China
Tel: +86-24-88622666
Fax: +86-24-88680777
Email: info@dopress.com
Website: www.dopress.com

SP
SendPoints

Published in Asia in 2011 by
Sendpoints Publishing Co., Limited
Room C, 15/F Hua Chiao Commercial Centre,
678 Nathan Road, Mongkok, KL, Hong Kong
Tel: (86)-20-89095121,34108463
Fax: (86)-20-89095206
Email: info@sendpoint.com.cn
Website: www.sendpoint.com.cn

Distributed by
Guangzhou Sendpoints Books Co., Ltd.
Email: export@sendpoint.com.cn
Website: www.sendpoint.com.cn
Sales Manager: Peng yanghui (China), Limbo (International)
Add: No.17-19, Xin Bao Road,Haizhu District,Guangdong,China
Guangzhou Tel: (86)-20-89095121
Beijing Tel: (86)-10-84139071
Shanghai Tel: (86)-21-63220892

Images (P228 - P253) copyright © 2011 Dopress Books
Cover and layout design copyright © 2011 Dopress Books

ISBN 978-988-18923-3-1
Hongkong Davinci Publishing Company Limited

DAVINCI

All rights reserved. No part of this publication may be reproduced, stored in any
retrieval system or transmitted, in any form or by any means, electronic, mechanical,
photocopying, recording or otherwise, without prior permission in writing from the
publisher. For information, contact Sendpoints Publishing Co., Limited or Dopress Books.

Printed and bound in China